NATIONAL
GEOGRAPHIC
KiDS

NERD ∧let

1.

1. (n.): a little book of nerdy stuff

1 2 3 4 5 6 7 8 9 10

ANIMALS

T. J. Resler

NATIONAL GEOGRAPHIC
WASHINGTON, D.C.

DUNG BEETLE, PAGE 148

INTRODUCTION

THIS BOOK ISN'T JUST ABOUT ANIMALS.

It's about passion, smarts, and expert knowledge. It's about knowing tons about animals and not being afraid to admit it. In short, it's about nerding out.

TERMITE, PAGE 72

If that sounds like you—or who you want to be—jump right in. This book is packed with weird and fascinating info about all kinds of animals. Some may be longtime favorites to you; others you've maybe never heard of. But all are amazing. You'll also find out how other animal nerds express their nerdiness, learn where to go to nerd out with some cool critters, and explore the ways animals appear in pop culture.

Take all that nerdy goodness and smoosh it into a portable package, and you've got *Nerdlet: Animals*, the book for people passionate about animals. In other words, the book for you.

WILD DANCE MOVES, PAGE 184

MAGICAL CATS, PAGE 170

REAL DRAGONS,
PAGE 10

Learn about this dog's do
on page 16.

PANGOLIN, PAGE 126

Check out notable noses of
the animal world on page 24.

5

RING-TAILED LEMUR

A MALE LEMUR PREPARES FOR AN ODOROUS ATTACK.

SURE, RING-TAILED LEMURS ARE CUTE, with their fluffy black-and-white tails and fuzzy ears. But don't be fooled: These cat-size primates from Madagascar can raise a real stink. Literally. When male lemurs get mad, they hurl stink bombs at each other! The lemurs rub their tails on scent glands on their wrists and chests, and then fling the stink at each other until one of them can't take it anymore and runs away. These little stinkers are so fond of throwing their scent around that they try to woo mates that way, too. Bad idea, dudes. The ladies often don't like the "stink flirting" and attack their smelly suitors. (Next time, try flowers.)

NERD ALERT: BEYOND BIZARRE

WE GET IT: Stink is important. A lot of animals rub their scent on stuff to mark their territories, warning others to stay away. Some animals—think stink bugs and skunks—use foul smells to defend themselves. But lemurs' stench warfare is in a class all its own.

FUN FACT

On chilly mornings, lemurs sit up, stretch their arms wide, and let sunlight warm their white bellies.

FUN FACT

Lemurs mark trees as their own with an acrobatic move. They do a handstand, grab the trunk with their feet, and wipe it with their scent from special glands on their bottoms.

ORCA

THE ORCA IS SUPERSMART. This marine mammal is huge—it can grow to be three quarters the length of a large school bus—and it has big brains to match. Take those smarts and add four-inch (10-cm)-long teeth, and you've got one of the world's top predators. Orcas don't just hunt; they work together to pull off sneaky attacks. They even figure out unique hunting techniques and teach them to their calves! Orcas have social relationships almost as complex as those of elephants and primates (like us). Up to 40 orcas live together in family pods led by the eldest female; each pod has a unique dialect of pulsed calls—patterns of sound and silence—whistles, and clicks. But get this, orcas can also learn to speak dolphin, which uses more clicks and whistles. Seriously smart.

FUN FACT

Members of a pod in Antarctica work together to hunt by making large waves that wash seals off the top of ice floes.

NERD ALERT: BRAINY BEHAVIOR

BRAINY OR BIZARRE? The orca comes by its smarts naturally. Its brain is the second biggest of all marine mammals, after that of the massive sperm whale. Its brain isn't just big in general: It's also big relative to its body size and very complex. Orca brains are extra wrinkly, which gives them more surface area—an indicator of intelligence. All signs of some serious brainpower.

DISTINCTIVE DRAGONS

THINK DRAGONS ARE ONLY THE STUFF OF FAIRY TALES AND FANTASIES? THINK AGAIN! THESE DRAGONS ARE THE REAL DEAL.

BLUE DRAGON

THIS BRIGHT, FRILLY DRAGON, a type of sea slug known as a nudibranch, floats along in the tropical and temperate waters of the Atlantic, Pacific, and Indian Oceans—thanks to an air bubble in its stomach. But beware: It can sting.

KOMODO DRAGON

THESE LIZARDS, NATIVE TO INDONESIA, grow as big as 10 feet (3 m) and 300 pounds (136 kg)—and eat pretty much anything they want. They lie in wait for unsuspecting prey and then pounce, biting down with knife-like teeth. Their bite is also venomous, causing their victims to go into shock and become totally helpless. Ouch!

SHOCKING PINK DRAGON MILLIPEDE

DON'T DIS THIS DRAGON because of its dinky size, which tops out at about an inch (3 cm) long. This spiky millipede, which lives in Thailand, isn't just crazily colorful; it's toxic. It protects itself by producing a poisonous acid, hydrogen cyanide.

FLYING DRAGON

THESE TEACUP-SIZE LIZARDS— also known as draco lizards—live in the jungles of Southeast Asia, where they fly from tree to tree. They have extra-long ribs that they can extend or retract at will, stretching out folds of skin to create wings. Capable of gliding up to 30 feet (9 m), they steer with their long, skinny tails and front legs.

HUMMINGBIRD

TWO FEISTY HUMMINGBIRDS FACE OFF

THE HUMMINGBIRD may only be the size of an adult human's thumb, but it packs a lot of mind-blowing awesomeness into its little body. This amazing athlete, which lives throughout the Americas, is the only bird that can hover in place for minutes at a time and fly backward with ease. Unlike most birds, its wings can move in every direction, even in a figure eight, allowing it to maneuver with precision. To power its flights, the hummingbird uses its forked tongue to lap up 10,000 calories of sugary nectar from 1,000 flowers every day. That'd be like you drinking a soda every minute of the day.

FUN FACT

Hummingbirds may be small, but they're tough. They chase other birds away from their territories—and we're not just talking other hummingbirds. They take on jays, crows, and even hawks.

NERD ALERT: BEYOND BIZARRE

HUMMINGBIRDS DON'T STAND OUT IN ONLY one category of bird-dom. They rack up honors in all sorts of extreme-animal categories: size, cuteness, strength, braininess, weird tongue-ness (it's a bigger category than you'd think). Any time you put so many standout features into one creature, it breaks into the ranks of the bizarre.

It's not like hummingbirds go around humming their favorite tunes. But they do create an audible hum by beating their wings up to 100 times a second.

13

DOG

DOGS AREN'T JUST our best friends, they're our students, too. These social animals learn from watching others do things. And get this, puppies don't just

A DOG SNIFFS AT A PUZZLE BOX.

learn from watching other dogs solve problems—they also learn from watching people! Researchers put some eight-week-old puppies to the test. They put tasty treats in a puzzle box and gave the puppies two minutes to figure out how to get at them. About half succeeded. Then the researchers did experiments during which the puppies got to watch either an adult dog or an adult human open the puzzle box. Afterward, the puppies got to try it themselves. They did much better—and it didn't matter if they had watched another dog or a person. It showed that dogs are great at adapting to and learning in different social environments. Good dogs!

FUN FACT

Dogs come in many shapes, sizes, and looks, but they're all considered one species (unlike, say, insects or fish). That makes dogs one of the most diverse species to walk Earth.

THE WAY DOGS go about solving problems also shows how attached they are to us. Dogs are decent problem-solvers, but if they get stuck, they stop trying to figure it out for themselves. Instead, they ask us for help!

FUN FACT

A border collie named Chaser learned the names of a thousand different things. Considered the world's smartest dog, she even learned the difference between "fetching" and "nosing" a toy—and much more.

TURN THE PAGE FOR MORE DELIGHTFUL DOGS—AND ONE HUMAN DEDICATED TO MAKING THEM SHINE.

15

Jess Rona grew up in a house with cats—not helpful when she got a job as a dog bather. One day her manager told her to put a lead (a type of leash) on a Lab, and she was, she admits, baffled. *Which is the Lab? Which is the lead?*

Fast-forward a couple of decades, and Jess can give you the deets on all kinds of dogs. Jess calls herself a "funny dog groomer," and she's become famous for both her signature grooming style and her humor.

For years, Jess groomed dogs by day and worked as a comedian and actor by night. Then Noodle came in for a clip, and Jess's world changed. As she was blow-drying the Pekingese, Noodle's ears flew up, making the pup look like a Hollywood star at a fashion shoot. Jess grabbed her phone and filmed the scene, then put music to it. "I realized it was the most fun thing ever."

Soon she was making lots of slow-motion music videos of her canine clients, showing off her unique grooming style in a way that's both glamorous and hilarious. She chooses songs that perfectly capture a dog's movements and, it seems, its emotions. After Jess started posting the videos on Instagram, they went viral, catapulting both Jess and the pups to fame.

"I never thought dog grooming was going to be a career, but I kept working this day job until it became my life. Now my two worlds are colliding, and it's magical."

JESS RONA, celebrity dog groomer, comedian

DIVING BELL SPIDER

THIS LITTLE AIR-BREATHING ARACHNID, which lives in Europe and northern Asia, has devised a clever way to stay underwater pretty much all the time. It lives, eats, and has its babies—all inside a bubble! The spider spins a web between underwater plants, and then fills it with air bubbles that it brought down from the water's surface on its tiny body hairs. Sometimes the spider just makes a bubble around part of its body, but it often makes one big enough to live totally inside it. Because there's more oxygen in the water around the bubble than inside the bubble itself, the bubble naturally draws in oxygen and pushes out the carbon dioxide that the spider exhales. So the air stays fresh, and the spider breathes easy.

NERD ALERT: COOL DIGS

WE GET IT: Spiders live in all kinds of places: deserts, forests, underground burrows, grasslands, maybe the corner of your room. But underwater? That takes some exceptional skill—and equally special digs.

FUN FACT

Air trapped on the diving bell spider's tiny body hairs lets the spider breathe while swimming around outside its bubble. It's like wearing a little scuba-diving suit!

FUN FACT

Back before people had scuba tanks, they explored the ocean using diving bells, hollow chambers that trap air inside—like if you turned a cup over and pushed it straight down into water. These apparatuses gave the spider its name.

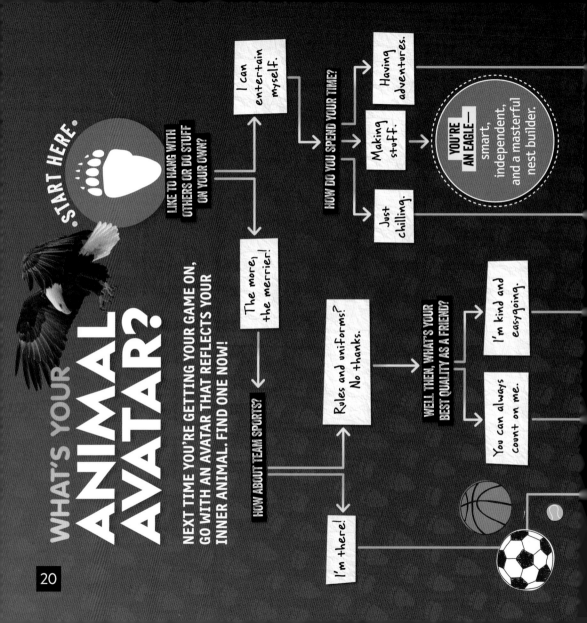

WHAT'S YOUR ANIMAL AVATAR?

NEXT TIME YOU'RE GETTING YOUR GAME ON, GO WITH AN AVATAR THAT REFLECTS YOUR INNER ANIMAL. FIND ONE NOW!

START HERE.

LIKE TO HANG WITH OTHERS OR DO STUFF ON YOUR OWN?

I can entertain myself.

The more, the merrier!

HOW DO YOU SPEND YOUR TIME?

Having adventures.

Making stuff.

Just chilling.

YOU'RE AN EAGLE— smart, independent, and a masterful nest builder.

HOW ABOUT TEAM SPORTS?

I'm there!

Rules and uniforms? No thanks.

WELL, THEN, WHAT'S YOUR BEST QUALITY AS A FRIEND?

I'm kind and easygoing.

You can always count on me.

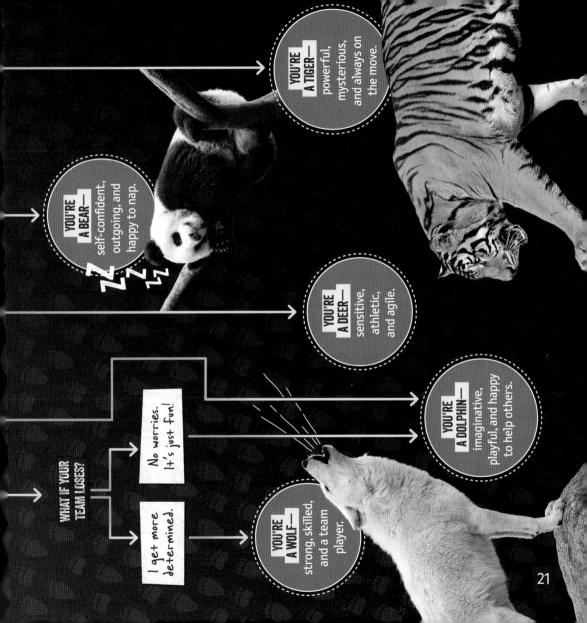

YOU'RE A TIGER— powerful, mysterious, and always on the move.

YOU'RE A BEAR— self-confident, outgoing, and happy to nap.

YOU'RE A DEER— sensitive, athletic, and agile.

YOU'RE A DOLPHIN— imaginative, playful, and happy to help others.

WHAT IF YOUR TEAM LOSES?

No worries. It's just fun!

I get more determined.

YOU'RE A WOLF— strong, skilled, and a team player.

21

ADÉLIE PENGUIN

IT MAY BE THE SMALLEST PENGUIN in Antarctica, but the Adélie has a supersize personality. The feisty little penguin will stand its ground, even driving away larger emperor penguin chicks with a barrage of flipper slaps. Sometimes it'll even battle potential predators, including large seabirds and seals. Male Adélies try to woo possible mates by building impressive nests lined with rocks. If they're not happy with the rocks they found, they'll steal some from their neighbors' nests.

FUN FACT

Early explorers to Antarctica had trouble figuring out what penguins were. First, they thought penguins were fish. Then they realized the error of their ways and decided they must be half fish, half bird!

AN ADÉLIE PENGUIN FEEDS ITS CHICKS.

BRAINY OR BIZARRE? Adélie penguins train to be feisty from an early age. When they're only about 11 days old, they begin grabbing each other's bills and feathers and slapping each other with their flippers. It's playful at that age, but it prepares them to tackle unknown adults or predators for real when they're only three weeks old.

FUN FACT

Adélie parents often lead their chicks on a wild chase before they regurgitate a meal of krill for the little ones. At first, many chicks— even those of other parents—come running for the food, but only the penguin's actual chicks will follow their parents for a long time. The other chicks give up.

NOSEY TYPES

MOVE OVER, PINOCCHIO. YOU'VE GOT NOTHING ON THESE CRITTERS, WHICH FEATURE SOME OF THE MOST SPECTACULAR SCHNOZZES IN THE ANIMAL KINGDOM.

LANTERNFLY

JUST CALL IT A SLURPY SNOUT. Some types of lanternflies, such as the *Pyrops candelaria*, grow a long, hollow "nose" that works like a combination spear and straw. The thirsty bug jams its snout into tree bark and sucks up sap. Despite the bug's name, its nose—or any other part of it—doesn't actually glow. But its wing patterns appear to shine in the light.

PROBOSCIS MONKEY

THIS MONKEY'S HUGE HONKER ISN'T JUST HANDSOME: Scientists think a male's large nose works as an echo chamber that amplifies his calls, including roars and—get this—actual honking noises to impress the ladies and scare off rival males. It works. Researchers found that the monkeys with the biggest noses had the most girlfriends.

ELEPHANT SHREW

BIG EYES AND EARS, POINTY LITTLE SNOUT—it's an adorable combination. But it's not just for looks. The elephant shrew's snout is long, flexible, and incredibly sensitive—perfect for helping it find and feast on ants, termites, berries, and the tender shoots of young plants. Not a true shrew, the little mammal is more closely related to elephants and aardvarks. The nose never lies.

ELEPHANT SEAL

ADULT MALE ELEPHANT SEALS ARE MASSIVE—think the size of a car—but they don't just rely on their size to scare off rivals. They inflate their trunk-like noses and make "clap-threats," deep *rat-a-tat-tat* drumming noises that can be heard a mile (1.6 km) away.

25

ARCHERFISH

ARCHERFISH LIVE IN THE WATER, just as you'd expect of any finny friend. But its favorite snacks—spiders, crickets, and other creepy crawlies—scamper around on branches and leaves out of reach. The solution to this problem? Great aim! An archerfish floats near the water's surface until it spies a tasty morsel. It sucks in a mouthful of water and blasts it out, knocking the bug off its perch. With excellent eyesight, its aim is precise, and its range is amazing. It shoots at prey five feet (1.5 m) above the water's surface. From the bug's perspective, it's like getting hit in the face with a Super Soaker—and then getting gobbled up.

NERD ALERT: FAB FOODIE

OK, MAYBE IT'S NOT *WHAT* they eat that earns archerfish the distinction of being fab foodies. But archerfish definitely secure their snacks with a style that's nothing short of fantastic. Even Robin Hood would be impressed.

FUN FACT

The scientific name of the banded archerfish (the most common kind) is *Toxotes jaculatrix*. *Toxotes* is from the Greek word for "archer," while *jaculatrix* is from the Latin for "javelin thrower."

FUN FACT

The archerfish doesn't just squirt water willy-nilly; it keeps changing the shape of its mouth to control the water blast so that it hits its target. This behavior may be similar to toolmaking in other species. Are fish smarter than we thought?

DESERT TORTOISE

THIS TORTOISE DEFINITELY NEEDS COOL DIGS. It lives in an area with blisteringly hot summers and frigid winters. But it has the perfect shelter for it. No, we're not talking about the big, domed shell on its back. The desert tortoise digs a burrow three to six feet (1 to 1.8 m) deep in rocky terrain. It hibernates in its burrow during the winter. Even in the summer, it heads inside and goes into a semi-sleepy state. It comes out to eat and drink only when the weather's nice, usually in the spring and fall. It's a strategy that works. Desert tortoises can live as long as 50 years in the wild.

FUN FACT

The desert tortoise spends as much as 95 percent of its life underground.

NERD ALERT: ⌊⌊⌊⌊⌊⌊**COOL DIGS**⌋⌋⌋⌋⌋

DIGGING IN THE ROCKY TERRAIN of the desert is no small feat, but the tortoise has strong forelimbs and sharp claws to create its digs. Good thing, because the Mojave Desert, in Utah, U.S.A., where the Agassiz's desert tortoise lives, can swing from 119°F (48°C) in August to only 8°F (-13°C) in January.

TEENSY TITANS

IMAGINE IF A NEW COMIC BOOK SERIES FEATURED ANIMALS WITH EXTREME POWERS. YOU MIGHT DISCOVER THAT SOME OF THE MOST AMAZING SUPERHEROES ARE THE ONES YOU SUSPECT THE LEAST.

SURVIVES **ANYWHERE,** EVEN **OUTER SPACE!**

SUPERHERO NAME:
WONDER BEAR

SECRET IDENTITY: Water bear (tardigrade)

SUPERPOWER: Nearly indestructible

SPECIAL MOVE: Curls into a ball to withstand radiation and temperature extremes

DANGER

RADIATION

DANGER

RADIATION

BLASTS INTO THE AIR AND POUNCES ON VILLAINS!

FLINGS ATTACKERS OFF HIM LIKE HE'S FLICKING AWAY DUST!

850 X MY WEIGHT

SUPERHERO NAME:
FLEANOMENON
SECRET IDENTITY: Flea
SUPERPOWER: Spring-like legs
SPECIAL MOVE: Jumps 50 to 100 times her body length

SUPERHERO NAME:
RADBUG
SECRET IDENTITY: Rhinoceros beetle
SUPERPOWER: Super strength
SPECIAL MOVE: Able to lift 850 times his weight

SEA OTTER

IT HOLDS HANDS WITH OTHER OTTERS, floats around on its back, and gives its babies rides on its belly. Sound the cute alarm! Yes, we're talking about the sea otter, the cuddly member of the weasel family that lives in coastal areas along the northern Pacific Ocean. It's not just expert at being adorable: It's crazy smart, too. It loves snacking on sea snails, crabs, and clams—which are all protected by tough shells, so the otter uses a tool to break in. While floating on its back, it puts a rock on its chest and smacks the shellfish on it over and over until it cracks open and reveals the tasty snack.

AN OTTER CRACKS OPEN A TASTY CLAM.

NERD ALERT: BRAINY BEHAVIOR

OTTERS FIGURED OUT how to use tools long before other marine mammals, including dolphins, according to recent research. Otters have probably been using tools for thousands, maybe even millions, of years—so long that it's become a natural behavior, not one they have to teach each other. That's some serious otter ingenuity.

HORSE

THE HORSE may not wag its tail or win our hearts with playful yips like dogs do, but it has its own way of communicating with us—we just haven't been paying much attention. Researchers studied how horses "told" people to get them a carrot in a bucket just out of the horses' reach. Each horse fixed its gaze on its person, touched them, and even pushed them toward the carrot. In other experiments, horses learned to press symbols on a display when they wanted their blanket put on or taken off. Others learned to touch a symbol on a computer touchscreen to get a carrot. That's a new kind of horsepower!

NERD ALERT: BRAINY BEHAVIOR

WE'VE KNOWN FOR A LONG TIME that horses are fast learners; that's what makes them fairly easy to train. Some recent experiments, however, reveal a whole new level of equine IQ. Horses even change the way they communicate with us based on what they think we already know.

FUN FACT

In the late 1800s, a horse named Clever Hans amazed people by tapping out answers to all sorts of questions with his hoof. Turns out, he didn't actually know the answers: He just stopped tapping when he sensed his trainer relax— at the right answer.

FUN FACT

Researchers have found that horses can tell the difference between smiling human faces and frowning human faces in photos.

WHAT GOOD CAN ANIMAL COMMUNICATION DO FOR PEOPLE? TURNS OUT—A LOT! CHECK IT OUT ON THE NEXT PAGE.

DO ANIMALS REALLY SENSE "BAD GUYS"?

It's lucky we humans have animals around. In a lot of stories, people are totally clueless when danger lurks. But not animals. They know who's bad, who's good, who's trustworthy, and who's not. How do they figure it out? They seem to have a sixth sense when it comes to judging people's character.

Is this just the creation of writers and moviemakers? Nope. Researchers are finding evidence for what we've long suspected: Animals can tell a lot about a person's character and intentions. Take dogs, for example. They generally give strangers the benefit of the doubt—kind of like "innocent until proven guilty." But if our pups see someone acting unkind toward us, they stop trusting them.

Researchers showed this with a simple experiment. They had a dog's person ask a stranger for help. If the person did indeed help out, the dog treated the stranger like any other person (meaning they were happy to take a treat from them). If the stranger refused to help, however, the dog gave them the cold shoulder. It even refused their treats. (That's really serious in dog-dom!) Trust broken. The same thing happened with capuchin monkeys. So you can rest easy knowing that some animals really do have our backs!

FUN FACT

Dante, the loyal canine in the movie *Coco*, was inspired by dogs called *xoloitzcuintli* (or "xolo"). Ancient Maya and Aztec believed that these dogs guided spirits safely to the afterlife.

TASMANIAN DEVIL

IT'S A SERIOUS UNDERSTATEMENT to say that the Tasmanian devil likes food. It throws itself into eating with a ferocity that's hard to imagine, growling and screeching at other devils that come to share the feast. In only half an hour, a Tasmanian devil can eat about 40 percent of its body weight. (That'd be like you eating 150 jumbo hot dogs—a seriously bad idea.) After gorging itself, the devil can barely waddle around. This Australian marsupial (pouched animal) isn't a picky eater either. It'll hunt small mammals and birds, but mainly it scavenges almost anything lying around—no matter how old. With its powerful teeth and jaws, it even eats the bones.

A NOISY DEVIL FEAST

NERD ALERT: FAB FOODIE

MAYBE "FAB" ISN'T THE BEST WAY to describe the Tasmanian devil's eating manners. But there's no doubt that this critter is passionate about feasting. It'll travel as far as 10 miles (16 km) for a meal, and it'll stuff itself so full that its tail swells with fat.

FUN FACT

When Tasmanian devils confront each other, their ears flush red. So, when early European settlers saw red-eared animals that had sharp teeth and made scary screeching noises, they dubbed them "devils."

39

SEA GOOSEBERRY

IT MIGHT NOT BE BIG ON BRAINS, but the sea gooseberry is brilliant in another way: It produces its own light show! As it drifts through the water, this transparent, jelly-filled oval—a type of comb jelly—sends pulses of light rippling along eight "comb-rows" that circle its body. The comb-rows, which act like tiny paddles, scatter the light into all the colors of the rainbow. Despite its delicate looks and small size, the sea gooseberry is a voracious predator—if you happen to be a tiny crustacean, like krill, that is. When its two long tentacles snag prey, it reels it in and spins, bringing the food close to the comb-rows, which carry it to the creature's mouth.

THE COMB-ROWS PUT ON A LIGHT SHOW.

NERD ALERT: Smart Style

A SEA GOOSEBERRY IS EYE-CATCHING in so many ways. First, there's the see-through body. Add to that the neon light show flashing along its sides, and you've got one stylin' sea creature. As for the "smart" part, the sea gooseberry doesn't understand how good-looking it is. Like jellyfish, a sea gooseberry doesn't have a brain like we usually think of them. Instead, it has a network of nerves that sense its surroundings.

40

FUN FACT

Sea gooseberries are both male and female at the same time.

A SEA GOOSEBERRY CHOWS DOWN ON A KRILL.

FUN FACT

Unlike their jellyfish relatives, sea gooseberries do not sting. Their tentacles are covered with a sticky goo to make sure prey doesn't get loose.

NERDSVILLE CENTRAL: BIG MAJOR CAY

4 TIPS TO NERD OUT WITH THE PIGS:

1 The only way to get to Big Major Cay is by boat.

2 The earlier you arrive, the better. By late afternoon, the pigs are pooped and mainly lounge on the beach.

42

WELCOME TO PIG BEACH

SOME PIGS PREFER TAKING A DIP in crystal clear water to wallowing around in the mud! Pig Beach—also known as Big Major Cay—is an island in the Exumas, a chain of tiny Bahamian islands with white sand beaches surrounded by clear turquoise waters. The island is inhabited only by feral pigs. No one is quite sure how they got there. Local lore says they swam ashore after a shipwreck decades ago or were dropped off by sailors who intended to come back for a big pig roast but never did. Whew! However they got there, one thing is clear: Tourists love them—and the little porkers love the tourists. They'll swim out to greet visiting boats, paddle alongside swimmers, and follow them down the beach. For pig lovers, this is paradise.

3 The pigs—some of which are huge—chase people who have food, so it's best not to eat on the beach.

4 If you want to see other animals, nurse sharks and iguanas live in nearby areas.

43

PUFFER-FISH

A MALE pufferfish makes some of the most awesome artwork you'll ever see in nature. The fish, which lives in the ocean near Japan, carves ornate circular ridges into the sandy seafloor without rest for seven to nine days. Reaching widths of seven feet (2 m), the patterns look a bit like giant, petaled flowers. The pufferfish even decorates the ridges with shells and then covers the design with a fine sediment to give it a distinctive look and color. Why all the work? The fish is trying to win the heart of a potential mate.

THIS PUFFERFISH DESIGN IS A "LABOR OF LOVE."

NERD ALERT: COOL DIGS

OTHER FISH MAKE CRATER-SHAPED MOUNDS for their mates, but none of them come close to the artistic mastery of the white-spotted pufferfish. The ridges, the shell decorations, and the dusting of fine sediment are all the signature style of this fish.

45

ROCKIN' ON!

OK, THESE CREATURES DON'T BLAST TUNES, BUT THEY DO A GREAT IMPERSONATION OF A ROCKER ... UM, SCRATCH THAT ... OF A ROCK.

WOLF SPIDER

THIS SPIDER, COMMON ALL OVER THE WORLD, prowls around sandy surroundings on the hunt for its next meal. Its camouflage keeps it safe from predators and lets it sneak up on prey. When it gets close to an unsuspecting insect, it pounces—and enjoys a tasty meal.

STONEFISH

YOU WOULDN'T WANT TO PICK UP and toss this "rock." It's the most venomous fish in the world. It sits still on the floor of the Pacific and Indian Oceans—so still that algae grow on it!—until its supper (maybe a little fish or shellfish) swims by. Then—with no warning—gulp!

PIURE

THIS SEA CREATURE, found off the coast of Chile and Peru, not only looks like a rock, it moves like one, too—meaning, not at all. Inside a tough shell, its body is bright red, earning it the creepy nickname "bleeding rock."

SOUTHERN ROCK AGAMA LIZARD

SITTING ON A SPECKLED ROCK, this lizard—found mainly in southern Africa—may escape the notice of snakes and birds that would otherwise gobble it up. Unless, that is, it's a male looking for a mate. Then its head turns bright blue!

47

CRITTER HIGH
CLASS SUPERLATIVES

Most Likely to Be Famous

DESPITE THEIR MASSIVE SIZE—weighing up to 8,000 pounds (3,600 kg)—hippopotamuses are elegant swimmers, and they can match human speeds on land. There's no denying this African animal's standout traits. Just ask fans of Fiona, the ultra-famous hippo celebrity from the Cincinnati Zoo in Cincinnati, Ohio, U.S.A. The little hippo's face has graced T-shirts, magnets, and hats—she's even made an appearance on a popular talk show. With all that hippo charm, it's no wonder!

Don't forget us when you're famous!!

—xoxo A. G. Parrot

Thanks for being the
swim team MVP this year!
Have a great summer!

 Axolotl

Glasswing Butterfly, **86-87**

Three-Toed Sloth, **128-129**

African Gray Parrot **158-159**

Axolotl, **204-205**

HONEYBEE

BEES BOOGIE TO SHARE INFORMATION

YOU'VE GOT TO ADMIRE THE HONEYBEE. Not only does it rock that whole "busy as a bee" thing—a single bee may stop at a hundred flowers every time it goes out to collect pollen!—but it's also smart. Each bee learns how to collect pollen by watching other bees and by trying new techniques. (Too hard to get inside a flower? A bee will bite off the bottom and suck the pollen out!) Bees also remember where the best flowers are and tell other bees how to get to them. They give directions by doing a "waggle dance" along a pretend line. If they dance straight up, it means to head from the hive in the direction of the sun. Down means away from the sun, and left and right mean how far to either side. Then the bees do fast or slow loops to indicate how close the flowers are. The more times they do the dance, the better the source. Maybe we should start saying "brainy as a bee."

FUN FACT

Honeybees can recognize individual human faces and tell them apart.

NERD ALERT: BRAINY BEHAVIOR

BEES DON'T JUST FIGURE OUT how to get pollen from the best flowers, they communicate with each other by using symbols in their waggle dance (a quick loop = pretty close; a long loop = farther away). That's a crazy level of intelligence.

51

POP ART

YOU'D BE HARD-PRESSED TO FIND MORE STRIKING PATTERNS IN A MODERN ART MUSEUM! JUST TAKE A LOOK AT THESE WILD WORKS OF ART.

TIGER

A TIGER'S STRIPES HELP BREAK UP ITS OUTLINE when it's prowling through tall grasses, where patchy sunlight creates lots of shadows.

ZEBRA

WITH ALL THOSE STRIPES IN A ZEBRA HERD, it's hard to tell where one zebra starts and another one ends—and that makes it tough for predators to pick one out. Stripes may be like a zebra superpower, keeping them cooler, protecting them from bug bites, and possibly confusing predators. (Scientists aren't exactly sure.)

MARBLED POLECAT

WHILE ITS BLACK-AND-WHITE FACE MAY STAND OUT, the colorful patterns on the marbled polecat's body may help it blend in wherever it lives—whether sandy areas, mountain meadows, or riverbanks.

GIRAFFE

A GIRAFFE'S PATTERN isn't random. It's passed down from its mom—and scientists found that some patterns keep giraffe babies extra safe from predators, possibly because they're better camouflaged.

WITH THESE LOOKS, IT'S NO WONDER ANIMALS INSPIRE SO MUCH ART. JUST ASK THE NERD OF NOTE ON THE NEXT PAGE!

On a typical day,

you might find Matthew Rivera staring up at a giraffe, cutting out a little hat for his pet rabbit, or wearing a ridiculously short tie.

It's all for his art. Matthew illustrates kids' books, creating pictures to help tell the stories. A lot of his illustrations involve animals doing crazy things—a chameleon photobombing a monkey's snapshots, a tiger conducting an orchestra, dinosaurs doing yoga—but they look totally believable. That's because Matthew works hard to capture the animals' looks, character, and actions.

He does this by sketching animals at the zoo, where he can see how a monkey's tail flops around as it swings or what a giraffe's neck looks like from way below. He's also had his pet rabbit, Lizzy, model a captain's hat—very briefly—for a story about a seafaring rabbit.

Sometimes Matthew gets into a character's mind by doing what it does—like wearing his necktie much too short in order to feel a giraffe's frustration about loving a tie that doesn't fit, or doing yoga like a dinosaur would.

"It's not enough to go to the Museum of Natural History and sketch dinosaur fossils. I had to perform yoga. What does this position feel like? What would a *Diplodocus* feel like stretching its neck out for this pose?" As he kept falling over during a tree pose, it struck him that a *Triceratops* would fall, too—so he drew that.

Matthew has been drawing animals ever since he could first hold a crayon. He hopes his art will make other people love and care for them as much as he does.

"Going into this career, I knew that my focus was going to be around animals. I've always been a big animal lover, and they always appear in my work."

MATTHEW RIVERA, illustrator

BURYING BEETLE

THE BURYING BEETLE DOESN'T TUCK its babes into clumps of grass or leaves. It welcomes its squirming little larvae into the world with a special nursery: the remains of a dead animal. Delightful, eh? The beetle takes its responsibilities seriously. Using chemical-sensing antennae, it locates a small animal—like a mouse or bird—that died recently and drags it home to prepare the nest. True to its name, the burying beetle digs a hole in the ground, where it places its prize and then chews out a cozy spot for its youngsters. The female lays her eggs, which hatch about 48 hours later. As the larvae grow, they can chow down on their nursery.

NERD ALERT: BEYOND BIZARRE

WHERE DO WE EVEN BEGIN? Burying beetles have taken the idea of a "bed and breakfast" to new extremes. It may seem a little creepy, but it's all part of a natural process that recycles the remains of other animals. And it sure beats leaving them lying around.

A BEETLE FEEDS ITS LARVAE FROM THEIR RAT "NURSERY."

FUN FACT

A burying beetle prevents the dead animal from decaying too quickly by coating it with special fluids from its mouth and bottom.

FUN FACT

A burying beetle can transport a dead animal that's 200 times its size as far as three feet (1 m) by rolling the corpse into a ball, wiggling under it, and moving its legs like a conveyor belt.

VAMPIRES

YOU KNOW THE TALES: THEY ROAM THE NIGHT, FEEDING ON THE BLOOD OF INNOCENT VICTIMS. THEY'RE VAMPIRES AND, LUCKILY, JUST THE STUFF OF STORIES. OR ARE THEY? CHECK OUT THESE REAL-LIFE VAMPIRES—AND MAYBE WEAR GARLIC, JUST IN CASE.

VAMPIRE BAT

THIS MOUSE-SIZE LATIN AMERICAN BAT is the only known mammal to survive on blood—mainly from cows, pigs, horses, and birds. But it doesn't sink in its fangs and suck up blood. It gently nicks an animal and licks up the blood from the scratch.

VAMPIRE SQUID

THIS CREATURE isn't really a vampire or even a true squid. It's a totally unique animal. It drifts along, eating whatever food sinks deep into the ocean. But when it's startled, it kind of turns inside out—almost like Dracula throwing a cape over his head—and displays scary-looking spines.

VAMPIRE FLYING FROG

THIS SMALL BROWN FROG, native to Vietnam, swoops down from trees, thanks to webbing between its toes that helps it glide. That's not where it got its name, though. Its tadpoles have creepy-looking, sharp black fangs that hang down under their mouths—probably for breaking into eggs to eat.

VAMPIRE CRAB

WILD COLORS AND GLOWING YELLOW EYES give this little crab a cool, spooky look that would make Count Dracula jealous. The freshwater crab comes out at night to look for food—which can be pretty much anything. Except for blood.

59

STAR-NOSED MOLE

THIS ODD-LOOKING MAMMAL, which lives in moist soil and marshes in North America, is definitely the touchy-feely type. That big pink star at the end of its nose? It's supersensitive, with 22 tentacles, or rays, of varying lengths shooting out in every direction. As the mole tunnels through moist soil looking for worms or water bugs to eat, its rays are a blur of constant motion, tapping as many as a dozen different places in a single second. At the same time it's touching something, it's also smelling it. The rays even keep soil from going up the mole's nostrils!

NERD ALERT: Smart Style

THE FIRST THING YOU SEE when this little critter is heading toward you is a big pink star. It's not just a fashion statement; that bizarre appendage is packed with more than 100,000 nerve sensors wired to the mole's brain. That's definitely smart style.

FUN FACT

Behind one of the star's rays, the mole has tiny front teeth that work like tweezers to pluck tiny prey from the ground. The rays spread apart to let the teeth snag the snacks.

FUN FACT

Star-nosed moles can smell underwater by blowing out air bubbles and sucking them back into their nostrils.

WHAT ANIMAL-INSPIRED
HERO
ARE YOU?

IT'S HARD TO BEAT ANIMAL ABILITIES—
AND SUPERHEROES KNOW IT. CHANNEL
YOUR ANIMAL INSTINCTS AND FIND OUT
WHICH OF THESE HEROES YOU'RE LIKE.

START HERE.

HOW MUCH DO YOU WANT TO BE LIKE ANOTHER ANIMAL?

A lot! It'd be amazing.

WILLING TO MORPH INTO ONE?

I'm all in.

YOU'RE LIKE VIXEN,
who gains the abilities of any animal—past, present, mythical—using her Tantu Totem.

Wait ... what? I just want to do what they do.

I'm already cool, but I'm up for more powers.

HOW WOULD YOU GET YOUR POWERS?

Hard to decide.

Gadgets are great.

WILLING TO LEARN A LOT AND WORK OUT?

LIKE MYSTICAL OBJECTS?

Yes!

MUTATION?

BUG BITE?

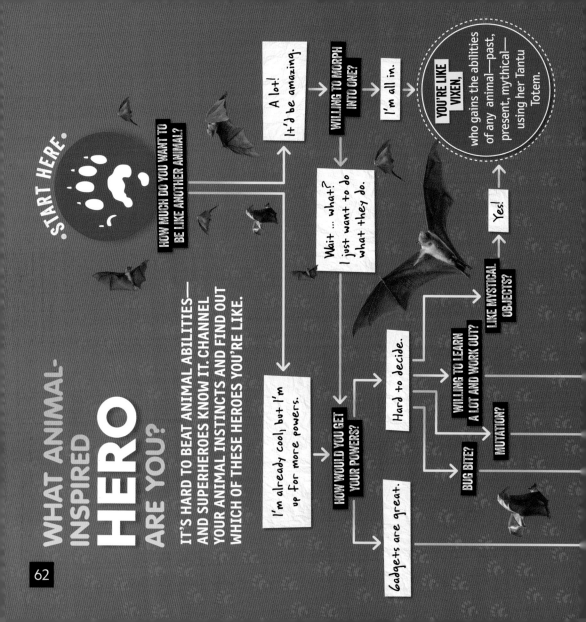

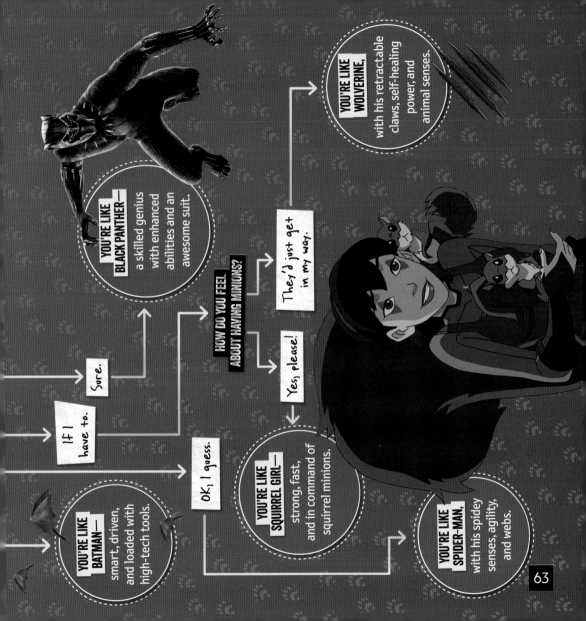

YOU'RE LIKE WOLVERINE, with his retractable claws, self-healing power, and animal senses.

YOU'RE LIKE BLACK PANTHER— a skilled genius with enhanced abilities and an awesome suit.

They'd just get in my way.

HOW DO YOU FEEL ABOUT HAVING MINIONS?

Yes, please!

Sure.

If I have to.

OK, I guess.

YOU'RE LIKE BATMAN— smart, driven, and loaded with high-tech tools.

YOU'RE LIKE SQUIRREL GIRL— strong, fast, and in command of squirrel minions.

YOU'RE LIKE SPIDER-MAN, with his spidey senses, agility, and webs.

NURSERY WEB SPIDER

A FEMALE SPIDER CARRYING AN INSECT SNACK

A MALE nursery web spider sure knows how to woo a mate—or so it seems. The fastest way to a female spider's heart is to give her a nice juicy bug to eat. So, the male spider traps an insect, wraps it up in his beautiful silk, and presents it to the female. If she likes the gift, she agrees to be his mate. But sometimes a male can't catch a bug—and he doesn't dare approach a female empty-handed. So he gift wraps a pebble or other worthless item and tries to trick the female.

NERD ALERT: BEYOND BIZARRE

IT'S ALWAYS A NICE IDEA to give a gift to someone you have a crush on. But for nursery web spiders, it's a necessity. The female spiders won't even look at a dude that doesn't have a gift. But wrapping up a bit of junk and pretending it's something great is not cool. It's just weird.

FUN FACT

Nursery web spiders get their name from the mother spider's habit of building a protective tent around her egg sac. She stands guard outside the nursery to protect her babies from predators.

FUN FACT

Nursery web spiders don't spin webs to trap food. They're hunters—and fast ones. When they see flies or other bugs nearby, they sprint to catch them.

A MALE SPIDER (FAR LEFT) MAKES HIS APPROACH

BETTA

PET BETTAS ARE MORE COLORFUL THAN THEIR WILD RELATIVES.

DON'T LET ITS SILKY, flowing fins fool you. This fish is tough. Native to Southeast Asia, it lives in shallow waters—rice paddies and river basins—that are still or slow-moving. During the dry season, streams may almost dry up. But bettas can handle it. They can live briefly in shallow puddles, thanks to a special ability to gulp in air from above the water's surface. They can also jump out of a puddle to deeper water nearby. Bettas don't like to share their territory, and this can create problems when they're kept as pets.

FUN FACT

A male betta creates a nest made of air bubbles held together by his saliva. He carries a female's eggs to the nest and guards them until they hatch.

NERD ALERT: BEYOND BIZARRE

TOUGH IS GREAT when it means surviving in less-than-ideal conditions, like a muddy puddle. These fish, formerly known as Siamese fighting fish, are territorial to the extreme. They chase other fish away and may even battle their own reflections in a fish tank wall.

PEOPLE LOVE THEIR PETS ... BUT DO THEY REALLY *KNOW* THEM? TURN THE PAGE TO FIND OUT.

DO PETS REALLY HAVE A SECRET LIFE?

Who hasn't wondered what their pets are up to when they're alone? If you believe movies and TV shows, our mild-mannered pups and kitties either sneak off on wild adventures—maybe even as detectives or heroes—or become true party animals. Any pet owners who've come home to trash strewn around the floor or pillows ripped apart may suspect their pets really were having a rollicking good time. The truth is more complex. Sure, lots of dogs and even some cats like to scavenge tasty morsels from the trash. But sometimes pets make a mess when they're stressed about being left alone. Dogs are definitely social animals, and cats—no matter how independent they act—like your company, too. They'd rather be with you, but they can get used to being on their own. Having safe, challenging puzzle toys can keep them from getting bored, and cozying up with one of your worn T-shirts may make the time apart easier. If the pets are content—and get enough attention, exercise, and mental stimulation when you're around—they'll probably sleep a lot of the time they're alone. So, the best sign that your pets are having a good time when you're out is ... nothing. No mess. No wild parties.

Of course, if they're really undercover secret agents, they'd be able to cover their tracks.

FUN FACT

Still convinced your pet is up to something? Inventors have created hi-tech pet cams that can help humans check in on their pets throughout the day. Some even dispense treats remotely.

FREAKY FLYERS

BIRDS AND BUGS AREN'T THE ONLY ANIMALS ZIPPING AROUND OVER OUR HEADS.

FLYING SNAKE

YIKES! Snake attack from above? Actually, a flying snake is probably just fleeing a predator. It jumps off a branch, flattens its body to about twice its normal width, and glides, steering by wiggling back and forth.

FLYING SQUIRREL

THE ORDINARY-LOOKING New World flying squirrel has a surprising trait—and it's not just gliding. It flashes hot pink in ultraviolet light. The pink fluorescence may help the squirrels identify each other or scare away predators.

FLYING FOX

THIS MEGA-BAT—also called a fox bat—has a wingspan that can reach five feet (1.5 m). It eats fruit and navigates by sight, not echolocation. Bats are the only mammals that can sustain powered flight, and a mom flying fox even flies with its newborn clinging to her belly.

A FLYING SQUIRREL GLIDES THROUGH THE AIR.

SUGAR GLIDER

THIS PALM-SIZE MARSUPIAL— a pouched animal, like the kangaroo—glides by stretching a thin skin between its front and back legs and steers using its bushy tail like a rudder. It can glide as far as 164 feet (50 m)— almost half the length of a football field.

71

TERMITE

WE USUALLY THINK OF THE TERMITE AS A PEST that destroys our homes—not as a master architect capable of constructing its own. A certain type of termite that lives in Australia, Asia, and Africa, however, builds massive mounds from mud, soil, and its own spit and poop. The mounds—which are like termite cities inside—can reach 30 feet (9 m) in height. The most impressive thing about the mounds is not their size though; it's how they keep the termites inside comfortable. The walls are porous—punctured by little holes that let in air. A network of tunnels and chimneys mixes the outside air with the air already inside, keeping it fresh and just the right temperature.

NERD ALERT: COOL DIGS

THESE TERMITE MOUNDS ARE SUCH IMPRESSIVE STRUCTURES that professional architects—the human kind—are modeling cutting-edge designs inspired by them. Termites have taught people how to make large buildings that use energy wisely. Definitely cool.

NERDSVILLE CENTRAL: CHINCOTEAGUE AND ASSATEAGUE ISLANDS

1 The ponies really are wild. They may kick or bite if you get too close, so don't try to pet, hug, or feed them.

2 The best way to see the ponies is by boat! You can take boat tours or rent kayaks to see them.

LAND OF WILD PONIES

MISTY OF CHINCOTEAGUE, the pony made famous by author Marguerite Henry, was real. If you want to see where she was from, just head to Assateague Island, near the town of Chincoteague, Virginia, U.S.A. Bonus: It's wild pony central! More than a hundred feral Chincoteague ponies still live on Assateague, an island split between the U.S. states of Virginia and Maryland. They roam freely along the beaches and munch on coarse dune and marsh grasses. Local legend has it that they're the descendants of Spanish horses shipwrecked off the coast back in the 16th century. There are actually two herds separated by a fence: one in a wildlife refuge in the Virginia part of Assateague and another (called Assateague horses) farther north in a national park on the Maryland side. Both areas have great beaches, natural shoreline, and hiking and biking trails, but it may be easier to see the ponies on the Virginia side.

4 TIPS TO NERD OUT WITH THE PONIES:

3 The charming town of Chincoteague, Virginia (which is on an island also called Chincoteague), is a few hours' drive from Washington, D.C., Philadelphia, and New York City.

4 Biking through the refuge in Virginia is a great way to see other wildlife, including eagles, ospreys, herons, and other birds.

ARCTIC FOX

THE ARCTIC IS A TOUGH PLACE TO LIVE. It's rocky and barren with blustery cold temperatures that can plunge to minus 58°F (-50°C) in the winter. But the arctic fox can take it. Its thick fur—including on its paws—helps keep it warm and camouflages the fox so it can hunt. In the snowy winter, the arctic fox is white. Come spring, its coat turns brown or gray. The arctic fox is very skilled at finding food. When it hears prey scurrying deep beneath the snow, it leaps high into the air and dives headfirst into the snow to catch its meal.

A FOX DIVES FOR ITS NEXT MEAL.

NERD ALERT: BRAINY BEHAVIOR

ARCTIC FOXES SHOW THEIR SMARTS by doing whatever it takes to stay well-fed in the harsh Arctic winter. When the going gets really tough, they let polar bears do the hard work of catching prey. The foxes just clean up afterward. That way, they save their energy and still get a decent meal.

FUN FACT

Compared to some other foxes, the arctic fox has a rounder body and shorter ears, muzzle, and legs. The compact build minimizes the amount of its body exposed to the cold. Plus, it can throw its bushy tail over its nose when it curls up.

FUN FACT

Arctic fox couples stay together for life, and both parents raise their pups.

SNUGGLY TYPES

WHETHER THEY LOOK HUGGABLE OR NOT, THESE ANIMALS ARE BEST BUDDIES WHEN THEY CURL UP TOGETHER INSIDE THEIR BURROWS.

RABBIT

THERE'S A REASON they're called snuggle bunnies. A rabbit sometimes lives with several other rabbits in a warren, a maze of underground tunnels and chambers, including special nursery nests. Babies—called kits, not bunnies (sorry)—are born hairless, so they snuggle together to keep warm, often changing places so each kit gets a turn in the toasty middle.

WARTHOG

LOOKING AT ITS SHARP, CURVED TUSKS, you might not suspect that the warthog likes to huddle together with others inside their burrows. Well, at least the females do. The males, or boars, are loners. But the females, or sows, are so sociable that they'll even share nursery burrows with other sows and piglets.

MEERKAT

SEVERAL FAMILIES of these sociable, squirrel-size African animals live together in large groups—called gangs or mobs—of up to 40 individuals. They spend a lot of time playing together, teaching younger members how to forage, and grooming each other. After a day spent outside, they snuggle together in their burrows.

BURROWING OWL

WHO NEEDS A TREE? Pairs of these little owls nest underground in burrows, often in a community near other burrowing owls. Even outside their nests, pairs may perch together, cooing to each other and rubbing their heads together. *Awww.*

79

AMERICAN RED SQUIRREL

THIS LITTLE TREE SQUIRREL HAS A SWEET TOOTH. Like other tree squirrels, the red squirrel chows down on conifer seeds, pine cones, nuts, berries, and pretty much anything it can get its paws on. It also stashes away food to get it through the winter, when pickings are scarce. It buries nuts and seeds here and there and piles many others in a heap, called a midden. But what sets the red squirrel apart is its love of syrup! When its seed stockpiles run low, the squirrel bites small holes through the bark of maple trees. After the tree sap drips out, runs down the bark, and dries, the squirrel comes back and licks up the sweet treat.

NERD ALERT: FAB FOODIE

SUGAR IS AN ENERGY SOURCE FOR BODIES—as your parents can surely tell you. So tapping maple trees at the end of winter is a great survival strategy for squirrels. The syrup gives them a boost of energy when they really need it. Besides, after a long winter of nothing but nuts and seeds, it makes a great dessert.

81

FUN FACT

Squirrels can sniff out buried seeds even under 30 inches (76 cm) of snow. Sometimes they forget where to sniff though, and the buried seeds grow into new trees—helping replenish forests.

SOCIABLE WEAVER

THEY LOOK LIKE ORDINARY brown, sparrow-size birds, but sociable weavers are among the most amazing architects in the world. They don't just make a little nest for a pair of them and their eggs. They build an entire apartment building where a colony of five to a hundred or more sociable weaver pairs live together. It looks like a big thatched hut hanging high up in a tree or on a pole. They build the roofs with large twigs and use grasses to make separate melon-size apartments, which they line with cozy materials, such as downy plant material, cotton, fur, and fluff. Generation after generation of birds work on the homes, adding and remodeling apartments.

THIS APARTMENT COMPLEX IS FOR THE BIRDS.

NERD ALERT: COOL DIGS

SOCIABLE WEAVERS ARE THE ONLY BIRDS to build such large communal homes. These massive homes provide insulation from the temperature extremes of the Kalahari and Namib deserts of southern Africa, where the birds live. Plus, extra community members are always around to help care for the babies.

IF ALL THIS BIRD STUFF HAS YOUR HEAD IN THE CLOUDS, YOU'VE GOT SOMETHING IN COMMON WITH THE NERD OF NOTE ON THE NEXT PAGE.

French photographer Christian Moullec is a bird nerd. He loves birds—especially geese—so much that he's earned himself the nickname "the Birdman." For many years, he watched birds waddling on the ground, swimming in lakes, and flying overhead on their annual migrations. Then he got worried.

Flocks of a certain type of goose, called the lesser white-fronted goose, were having trouble migrating from Germany to Scandinavia, farther north, and so their numbers were dwindling. Conservationists started working to reintroduce more birds to that habitat. Christian wanted to help, so he began raising orphaned geese. Then he took to the air. He adapted a microlight aircraft—a lightweight aircraft that looks like a tricycle attached to a hang glider and propeller—and learned to fly. He flew along with the geese, guiding them on their migration.

Flying within an arm's reach of the birds as they wing their way across the sky is a really special experience for Christian, and he wants to share that feeling with others. He films his flights with the wild birds in hopes that the beautiful images will move people to help protect them. He also gives rides to tourists to raise money for conservation efforts.

It'd be fair to say that Christian takes nerdiness to new heights. Literally.

"The most beautiful thing to realize on Earth is to fly in the heavens with the angels that are the birds."

CHRISTIAN MOULLEC, the Birdman

I love your style! #goals

♥ Hippo

CRITTER HIGH
CLASS SUPERLATIVES

Most Fashionable

VIBRANT COLORS. Bold lines. Crystal clear wings. The glasswing butterfly truly looks like a work of art. Its see-through wings have fashion and function: They help the butterfly evade predators by easily blending into their surroundings. The stylish insect has even inspired humans to improve their own lives. Scientists studied the butterflies' wings to develop a high-tech, water resistant type of glass. *Très chic!*

Sometimes I look right through you, but you're still my favorite fashionista. See you next year!

—xoxo A. G. Parrot

Hippo, **48-49**

Three-Toed Sloth, **128-129**

African Gray Parrot **158-159**

Axolotl, **204-205**

ELEPHANT

SWEET AND SMART may not be the first thing you think when you see this powerful pachyderm. But the elephant, the largest living land animal, is an intelligent and gentle giant that lives in complex communities led by an experienced female, or matriarch. Related mothers and children stay together in a herd all their lives. They work together, protect each other's babies, and consult each other on important decisions. It's not just a survival strategy. Elephants really seem to feel for one another. They often don't leave sick or injured elephants behind, and they even try to calm down upset herd members by stroking them with their trunk.

NERD ALERT: BRAINY BEHAVIOR

WE'VE ALWAYS KNOWN that elephants have great memories. The matriarch can remember where the best watering holes are for years—even when they're nowhere close. Scientists are now realizing that elephant smarts go far beyond that. They use tools, communicate in all sorts of ways, and, unlike many other animals, can even recognize themselves in a mirror.

FUN FACT

The elephant trunk is a lips-and-nose combo with agile "fingers" at the end. It's strong enough to push down trees and sensitive enough to pick up a single blade of grass.

FUN FACT

Talk about teeth! Tusks actually are an elephant's long incisors—used for digging, lifting, and defending itself. An elephant also goes through six sets of molars during its life.

SHRIKE

HOW WOULD A SWEET LITTLE SONGBIRD like this earn the nickname "butcherbird"? Just watch it tackle a meal and all will be made clear. This songbird has a chill-inducing way of hunting. It swoops down on an animal and, with a precise bite to its neck, pinches its spinal cord to paralyze it. Then the shrike whips its prey's head around hard enough to break the animal's neck. It doesn't end there. After carting its catch home, the shrike then skewers it on a thorn, twig, or even barbed wire.

NERD ALERT: BEYOND BIZARRE

YOU MAY NOT WANT shrikes to come visit your bird feeder, but you have to admit that these butcherbirds take their meals seriously. Not only are they ferocious predators, but their hunting style is unique, to say the least.

FUN FACT

A shrike eats bugs, lizards, mice, and small birds—sometimes creatures as large as it is.

FUN FACT

Sometimes shrikes leave their prey skewered on a stake for a while— until it starts to rot and becomes easier to pull apart.

MILDLY MIFFED BIRDS

IMAGINE THE EPIC GAME ANGRY BIRDS GOT A NEWER AND, WELL, LESS ANGRY VERSION. THESE REAL-LIFE ANIMALS—AND WANNABE GAMERS—MIGHT TRY OUT TO BE SOME OF THE CHARACTERS.

CONTESTANT

1

LAWRENT THE LAMMERGEIER

STANDOUT FEATURE: Red-rimmed eyes, 9-foot (2.7-m) wingspan

SKILL: Smashing huge bones by dropping them on rocks

DEEP DARK SECRET: His reddish feathers aren't natural; they're dyed with mineral-rich soil or water.

SNIVELY THE SEAGULL

STANDOUT FEATURE: Boldness

SKILL: Flinging clams so hard their shells break

DEEP DARK SECRET: Steals from friends when they're not looking

CASSANDRA CASSOWARY

STANDOUT FEATURE: Helmet, bright wattles

SKILL: Able to spring, jump, and kick with dagger-like claws

DEEP DARK SECRET: Actually shy

BRADY "BAD BOY" BABIRUSA

STANDOUT FEATURE: Tusks growing out of the top of his snout

SKILL: Standing on his hind legs and boxing with front legs

DEEP DARK SECRET: Tusks are fragile and pretty useless

ORANGUTAN

IF THIS ORANGE APE looks like it's deep in thought, don't be surprised. It's seriously brainy. It builds or remodels sleeping nests every day and uses all kinds of tools. Correction: It doesn't just use tools; it makes them! Orangutans fashion branches and leaves into different shapes for whatever they need: scooping up bugs or honey to eat, scratching hard-to-reach itches, or even measuring the depth of water. In an experiment, they figured out how to bend wires to hook little treat-filled baskets that were put into a tube—and they did it better than a group of five- to eight-year-old human kids. Like humans, they also teach each other their group's traditions.

FUN FACT

Some orangutans make rain ponchos out of large leaves to stay dry in the rain.

NERD ALERT: BRAINY BEHAVIOR

THEY BUILD, THEY TEACH, THEY CRAFT TOOLS. Wait, there's even more! Orangutans are the only primates—besides us humans—to talk about the past. That's advanced stuff. In an experiment, orangutan moms saw a "threat" (a researcher in a tiger costume) and quietly whisked their kids to safety. Only after the threat was gone did the apes talk about it. Though safe, the apes' chat included the unique warning sounds they use for danger.

DENIZENS OF THE DARK

WHEN DARKNESS FALLS, THE DAY'S JUST GETTING STARTED FOR THESE NOCTURNAL ANIMALS.

AYE-AYE

THIS LITTLE LEMUR from Madagascar has fingers like E.T. and ears that would make Yoda jealous. It uses its long middle fingers to tap on trees and listen for hollow spots where insects may be hiding. Then it bites holes in the bark and spears grubs and other bugs with a sharp claw.

COYOTE

KNOWN SOMETIMES AS THE "SONG DOG," the coyote makes all sorts of sounds—including yips, growls, barks, and howls—but it's best known for the yip-howling it does in a group. This extremely adaptable and clever member of the dog family, native to prairies and deserts, now lives everywhere, including in cities.

RACCOON

THIS CUTE, MASKED ANIMAL is a handy critter—quite literally. Its front paws have five toes that act a lot like our fingers. It is quick enough to snatch crayfish out of water or mice out of hiding places. It lives in all sorts of places, and there may now be more raccoons living in cities than in the countryside.

WOLF

THAT LONE MOURNFUL HOWL? It's a wolf, but it's not howling at the moon. It's getting the attention of its pack, a tight group of about eight other wolves led by an alpha male and female pair. Each wolf's howl is unique—kind of like our own voices.

NOCTURNAL ANIMALS OFTEN GET A BAD RAP.
JUST CHECK OUT THE FURBALLS ON THE NEXT PAGE.

ARE HYENAS REALLY SNIVELING, EVIL VILLAINS?

In stories, hyena characters are sometimes just plain silly—that whole "laughing hyena" thing. More often, though, they're portrayed mean, greedy, cowardly, and willing to do anything for a scrap of food. Especially if it means stealing from noble lions.

Hyenas' bad-guy reputation goes back thousands of years. Africans viewed them as greedy and powerfully dangerous, but also stupid and comical. Europeans thought hyenas lived near graves, digging up buried bodies to eat, or that they used human-like sounds to lure victims to their deaths. Some thought they practiced witchcraft or even possessed the souls of the dead.

Could any of this be true? Hyenas are definitely weird. Their strange calls—long whoops and high-pitched giggles—can be kind of creepy. But the animals actually evolved a range of sounds to communicate with each other. They're smart and, admittedly, sometimes sneaky. If a hyena can't get to a meal, it may sound an alarm that danger's near— even if it's not—so the other hyenas run away, leaving it to eat. And about that meal? Most of the time, hyenas work together to catch their own prey instead of scavenging it from other animals, such as lions. That doesn't mean that if they find meat lying around, even if it's rotting, they're not happy to get an easy snack. They eat every bit—bones and all—so they're kind of like nature's cleaning crew.

FUN FACT

Spotted hyenas live in complex matriarchal—or female-led—groups called clans.

HA!

HA!

HA!

HA!

HA!

HA!

HA!

HA!

HA!

HA!

HA!

99

OKAPI

IGNORE THE ZEBRA STRIPES and horsey-ish body for a minute. If you could make an okapi stick out its tongue and say *ahhh*, you might notice similarities between it and another well known creature, the giraffe. You can see the resemblance in the shape of its head and definitely in its dark tongue, which is 14 to 18 inches (36 to 46 cm) long. So why does its body look so different? Okapis live in the African rainforest—not on wide-open savannas like giraffes—so they need short necks to duck under tree branches. And those stripes? Great camouflage for a rainforest, where only streaks of sunlight break through the leaves.

NERD ALERT: Smart Style

THE OKAPI'S BUILD AND STRIPES are perfectly suited to its rainforest habitat—and it's an eye-catching look (to us, but not to predators). The stripes may even help okapi babies find their moms in the dark forest.

FUN FACT

The okapi has scent glands on its feet that leave behind sticky, smelly markings as it walks around its territory.

FUN FACT

Okapis—the giraffe's only living relative—are also known as forest giraffes.

101

NERDSVILLE CENTRAL: CHENGDU PANDA BASE

1 Pandas are more likely to sit out in the open between September and June, when the weather is cooler.

2 Panda lovers come from all over to visit this place, so get there early on a weekday to beat the huge crowds.

3 Panda moms usually give birth from July through September, so that's the best time to see newborns.

✈ PANDA LOVER'S PARADISE

GIANT PANDAS. LOTS OF THEM. Babies, toddlers, families. Need we say more? If you want to get close to what may be nature's cutest creatures, there's no place better than Chengdu Panda Base in China's Sichuan province. It's a huge park—more than twice the size of Disney World's Magic Kingdom—and is home to roughly 175 pandas. The park is dedicated to conservation, research, and education about these adorable and rare black-and-white animals, which start off their lives the size of a stick of butter. Though you can't touch the animals, you'll get close enough to hear the sound of them munching bamboo. You can see mothers nursing babies and panda toddlers playing with each other. Chengdu is in an area where pandas live in the wild, and the panda base works to re-create that environment with bamboo forests, streams, lakes, rocks, and caves—great playgrounds for pandas. Get ready for some serious panda-monium!

5 TIPS TO NERD OUT WITH THE PANDAS:

4 Panda Base is only about six miles (10 km) from the city of Chengdu, in Sichuan Province, so that's a great place to stay.

5 The park is also home to red pandas, swans, butterflies, and peacocks and other birds.

103

TEAR-DRINKING MOTH

OK, THIS IS JUST PLAIN RUDE. This moth slurps up the tears of birds, grazing cows, deer, and even crocodiles—animals that can't exactly reach up and shoo them away. It has a long tubular mouth part, called a proboscis, that's hollow like a straw. The moth pokes this proboscis onto an animal's eye and sucks up their tears. Some species of the moth even have little hooks that anchor their proboscis in place. *Ouch*. No one knows if it actually bothers the tearing animal. Still. Scientists haven't completely figured out why the moths do this, but it probably has more to do with getting nutrition than being despicable. The moths drink salty liquid wherever they can find it.

A MOTH PREPARES TO SLURP TEARS FROM A BLACK-CHINNED ANTBIRD.

NERD ALERT: FAB FOODIE

LOOK, WE DON'T MEAN TO THROW SHADE, but the whole poke-you-in-the-eye approach to getting a drink is pretty weird. Still, it's actually an ingenious way to suck up some nutrition. Tears have a lot of salt and a surprising amount of protein—essential nutrients for a balanced diet.

FUN FACT
Moths aren't the only critters that drink the tears of other animals. Some butterflies, bees, and flies do it, too.

TEAR-DRINKING MOTHS MUST LOVE THE BIG CRYBABIES ON THE NEXT PAGE.

Ever hear someone be accused of "shedding crocodile tears"? It means they're acting sad, but they're really just faking it. So what does that have to do with fearsome reptiles?

A long time ago, someone noticed crocodiles shedding tears while they devoured their prey. A 14th-century book called *The Voyage and Travels of Sir John Mandeville, Knight*—very popular in its day—put it this way: "There's a great plenty of crocodiles. These serpents slay men, and then eat them weeping."

Eat them weeping! What?! Here's the thing: Nobody really knows what emotions crocodiles feel while they're eating, but it's a pretty safe bet that they're not weeping over their victims. So, those tears? Obviously, observers might think that the crocs are faking their remorse.

The funny thing is that crocodiles really do shed tears when they eat. It's not an outpouring of emotion, though, but probably just a physical side effect of how they devour their meals. They often hiss and huff, pushing some air up through their sinuses to their tear ducts, making tears puddle.

PLATYPUS

A PLATYPUS MUCHES ON A CRAWFISH.

TAKE TWO PARTS DUCK, ONE PART OTTER, A BIT OF BEAVER—and a whole lot of imagination—and you just might dream up the platypus. Then again, maybe not. This truly unique Australian mammal glides through streams, propelled by its webbed front feet and steering with its partially webbed back feet and beaverlike tail. It's streamlined and has waterproof fur, like an otter, but forages for food very differently. Its duckbill contains electro-sensors that help it locate prey, such as insects and shellfish, which it scoops up from the bottom of the stream and stores in its cheek pouches. On land, it can retract the webbing on its feet to reveal claws—great for traction and digging burrows.

FUN FACT

They may look cute, but male platypuses are armed with serious weaponry. On their rear ankles, they have spiky spurs that can deliver a nasty dose of venom.

NERD ALERT: Smart Style

THIS ANIMAL IS SO UNUSUAL that it took scientists roughly 80 years to figure out what it was. Furry duck? No. Egg-laying mammal? Yes. In fact, back in the late 1700s and early 1800s, the first Europeans to see a platypus actually thought it was a prank! Now we know the platypus rocks a signature style all its own.

UNICORNS

NOT ALL UNICORNS ARE THE STUFF OF LEGEND! THESE ANIMALS ARE REAL ONE-HORNED WONDERS.

UNICORNFISH

YOU WON'T see a horn on a young unicornfish. The horn grows as the fish gets older, but, even then, it doesn't protrude beyond its snout.

GREATER ONE-HORNED RHINOCEROS

SOME RHINOS HAVE TWO HORNS, but this Indian rhino—the largest of the rhinos—boasts a single horn that can reach 8 to 24 inches (20 to 61 cm) long.

HELMETED CURASSOW

THE "HELMET" on this chicken-size South American bird is actually made of bone and covered in skin.

NARWHAL

THIS ARCTIC WHALE with its strange spiraled tusk—actually a tooth that can grow eight feet (2.4 m) long—may have inspired tales of fantastical sea creatures.

RED PANDA

THIS RED PANDA IS CURLED UP FOR A NAP.

THIS MISCHIEVOUS, cinnamon-colored animal is about the size of a large cat, and it's fluffy all over. It has a dense double coat—with woolly hairs close to its skin and longer coarse hairs on top. It even has fur on its feet. And it's hard to find a more impressive tail! Not only is this tail superstylish, with its alternating beige and red rings, but it comes in handy for all sorts of things. It helps a red panda keep its balance as the agile animal scampers from branch to branch. And when it's chilly outside, the panda can wrap itself in its bushy tail to stay nice and cozy and warm.

NERD ALERT: Smart Style

IT MAY NOT SEEM LIKE A FIERY red coat is good camouflage for a forest-dwelling animal, but it's perfect for the red panda's natural habitat, where the branches of fir trees are often covered with white lichen and clumps of reddish brown moss.

FUN FACT

Red pandas are only very distantly related to giant pandas. Like the large black-and-white pandas, red pandas also eat bamboo.

FUN FACT

The red panda can climb down trees headfirst, thanks to a really flexible ankle and lower leg that rotate backward.

BEAVER

"BUSY AS A BEAVER" IS NO JOKE. A master of engineering and architecture, this large rodent changes its habitat to suit it—an unusual thing for animals to do. Its teeth are strong and sharp enough to cut through a small tree or branch as thick as an adult human's finger in just one bite, and it gnaws around the bases of larger trees until they topple, too. Beavers then weave the branches, saplings, and logs together with reeds and packed mud to build watertight dams and dome-shaped lodges with underwater entrances and cozy indoor living spaces for their families. While a beaver works and swims underwater, valves in its ears and nostrils close to keep water out, and clear eyelids cover its eyes—kind of like swim goggles!

NERD ALERT: COOL DIGS

BEAVER LODGES LOOK LIKE LITTLE ISLANDS. They rise only a bit above water level, but they're often four feet (1.2 m) wide and two feet (0.6 m) high inside. Beavers think of everything: They leave an air hole—called a chimney—in the roof for ventilation and cover the floor with wood shavings to keep it dry and comfy.

FUN FACT

Beavers are about the size of a basset hound. They're the second largest rodent after capybaras, which live in South America.

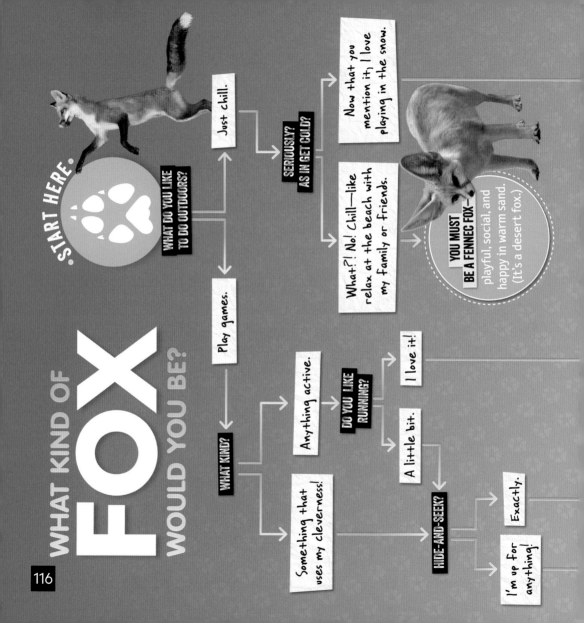

WHAT KIND OF FOX WOULD YOU BE?

START HERE.

WHAT DO YOU LIKE TO DO OUTDOORS?

Just chill.

SERIOUSLY? AS IN GET COLD?

Now that you mention it, I love playing in the snow.

What?! No! Chill—like relax at the beach with my family or friends.

YOU MUST BE A FENNEC FOX— playful, social, and happy in warm sand. (It's a desert fox.)

Play games.

WHAT KIND?

Anything active.

DO YOU LIKE RUNNING?

I love it!

A little bit.

HIDE-AND-SEEK?

Exactly.

I'm up for anything!

Something that uses my cleverness!

116

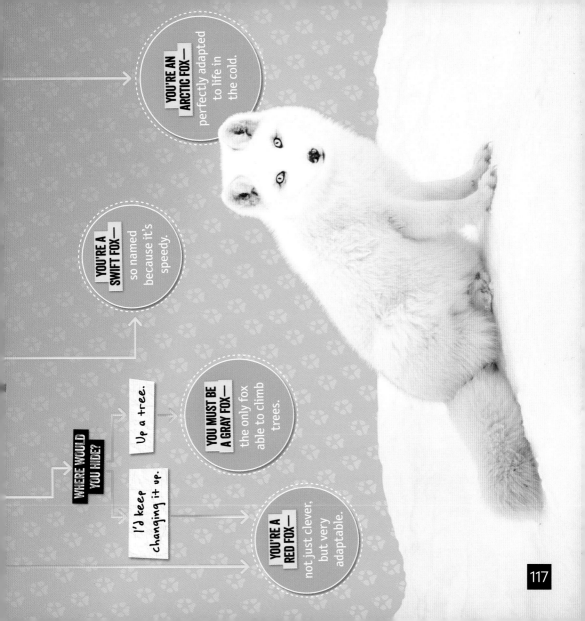

YOU'RE AN ARCTIC FOX— perfectly adapted to life in the cold.

YOU'RE A SWIFT FOX— so named because it's speedy.

Up a tree.

YOU MUST BE A GRAY FOX— the only fox able to climb trees.

WHERE WOULD YOU HIDE?

I'd keep changing it up.

YOU'RE A RED FOX— not just clever, but very adaptable.

117

SEA TURTLE

IF YOU NEEDED ANY PROOF of the amazing ways that animals adapt to their environments, just look at the sea turtle. Over millions of years, its legs evolved into flippers. It uses its front limbs like paddles to cruise along at speeds as fast as 15 miles an hour (24 km/h) and uses its hind limbs like rudders to steer. Like Crush in *Finding Nemo*, this marine reptile really does ride ocean currents to travel hundreds or thousands of miles. Guided by Earth's magnetic field, female sea turtles return to the same beach where they were born to lay their eggs—about 80 to 120 of them at a time!

NERD ALERT: BEYOND BIZARRE

ONLY ABOUT 100 KINDS OF REPTILES—out of roughly 12,000—live in the sea. That's not the only reason sea turtles are special, though. Their amazing adaptations really set them apart. For example, turtles get rid of excess salt in their bodies using a special gland near their eyes. It makes them look like they're crying!

Unlike other turtles, the sea turtle cannot pull its head and limbs into its shell.

There are seven types of sea turtles, each with unique features. Leatherbacks are the biggest, and green sea turtles are the only vegetarians. Hawksbills have bird-like beaks, and loggerheads have impressively large heads.

IT'S TOUGH TO REALLY CAPTURE ALL THE AWESOMENESS OF OCEAN ANIMALS, BUT THE NERD OF NOTE ON THE NEXT PAGE COMES REALLY, REALLY CLOSE.

Michael Aw is on a mission. He wants to inspire people to love Earth and all its animals, so he tells stories about these animals. And he uses a camera to do it.

Michael is a wildlife photographer who's most famous for his underwater pictures of marine animals. To get these pictures, he travels to remote places, dives into frigid waters, and faces down sharks. And he also waits. A lot. It can take years and many dives to capture the perfect moment—the one that reveals what an animal is all about. Michael doesn't just have great skill with a camera. He also learns all about animals—their behavior and where and how they live—and he has a lot of respect for them.

Michael's had many amazing moments photographing animals. He's touched a crocodile, had a shark come so close he had to push it away with his camera, and been lifted up by a whale. But the most unforgettable experience was when he and an assistant were photographing sharks—and one thought Michael might make a tasty snack. The photographers stayed far underwater, their air supply getting low, while the shark circled overhead. Suddenly, six dolphins came and shoved the sharks away and then led the photographers to safety. It was a perfect example, Michael says, of the special connection we share with animals.

sea turtle

120

"A photograph must tell a story, and that picture must thrill the senses and inspire that 'wow' factor. So we have to look out for that moment, look out for the story."

MICHAEL AW, wildlife photographer

coral filefish

coral shelf

whale shark

121

POLAR BEAR

THE BONE-CHILLING TEMPERATURES OF THE ARCTIC don't faze a polar bear. Sure, now and then it digs a pit in the snow to weather a blizzard or to get a night's sleep. Most of the time, though, it's out and about, protected by its thick fur and fat—unless it's about to have babies. A mother polar bear will dig a cozy den into a snowbank and spend the bitterly cold winter inside with her newborn cubs. The thick snow walls work like insulation, trapping the bears' body heat inside. It may be way below freezing outside, but the dens get as warm as 40°F (4.4°C)—nice and toasty for a polar bear.

NERD ALERT: COOL DIGS

TALK ABOUT COOL DIGS: These homes are made of snow! A mother polar bear digs a long tunnel that leads to an oval-shaped den just big enough for her to turn around in. Then, after her cubs are born, there may be a bit of remodeling, with the bears digging out additional small chambers connected by tunnels.

TOADALLY AWESOME

THESE ODDBALL AMPHIBIANS BREAK THE MOLD OF TOAD-DOM.

PEBBLE TOAD

THIS SMALL, BUMPY-SKINNED TOAD is a real rock-and-roller. When a predator approaches, it doesn't run or hide. It rolls up into a little ball and tosses itself down a mountain. But don't worry—the toad weighs so little that it survives the fall without a scratch.

SURINAM TOAD

HERE'S A NOVEL NURSERY: After a female Surinam toad lays her eggs, her mate rolls them onto her back, where her skin grows over them. When the eggs are ready to hatch, the toadlets pop out of holes on their mom's back.

MEXICAN BURROWING TOAD

DESPITE THE SPORTY RED STRIPES down its back, this toad isn't a racer. Its stubby legs are only built for burrowing. But when it calls out, it does sound a bit like a revving engine—an effort that makes its body puff up like a balloon.

PANGOLIN

NOPE, IT'S NOT AN OVERGROWN LIZARD. It's a mammal—a scaled mammal! Though it may not be fluffy cute, this shy creature has a streamlined style all its own. It's clad in tough, overlapping scales made of keratin. Keratin is the same stuff your fingernails are made of, and, like your nails, pangolin scales keep growing. They get filed down naturally when a pangolin tunnels through soil looking for termites and ants. When it finds its favorite meal, it laps them up with an amazingly strong, sticky tongue that is as long as its head and body combined. In fact, its tongue is too long to fit into its mouth; it retracts all the way inside the pangolin's chest!

PANGOLINS SOMETIMES WALK ON ONLY TWO LEGS.

NERD ALERT: Smart Style

PANGOLINS NOT ONLY LOOK COOL, they also have a super-stylin' move. When threatened, they roll up, presenting would-be predators with a tough, armored ball. Mothers will even ball up around their babies! No surprise that they get their name from the Malay word *peng-goling*, which roughly means "roller."

FUN FACT

Though pangolins are sometimes called "scaly anteaters"—thanks to their looks and diet—they're actually more closely related to your pet dog or cat than to anteaters or armadillos.

127

CRITTER HIGH
CLASS SUPERLATIVES

Most Likely to Be Late for Class

WHEN IT COMES TO BEING SLOW, three-toed sloths are in a class of their own. These sluggish sleepyheads snooze for a whopping 15 to 20 hours per day. And when they are awake, they spend most of their time hanging motionless from tree branches. The only way these critters might make it to class on time is if the school were in water. (Sloths are actually pretty good swimmers.)

You should really join the swim team next year.

—Axolotl

I hope you get even more rest than normal this summer. Stay chill!

♡ Glasswing B.

Hippo, **48-49**

Glasswing Butterfly, **86-87**

African Gray Parrot **158-159**

Axolotl, **204-205**

TRAPDOOR SPIDER

THIS ARACHNID DOESN'T HANG OUT on a web like other spiders. It spends most of its life underground in a burrow. But this isn't your average hole in the ground. These burrows—which can be one foot deep (30 cm) and two inches (5 cm) wide—have all the comforts of home. Each spider lines its burrow with silk and builds an actual door at the entrance. The door is made of leaves, moss, or whatever else is lying around outside—great camouflage—and is hinged with the spider's stretchy silk. The spider peeks out from beneath the door, waiting for prey to walk by.

THIS INVITING ENTRANCE LEADS TO A SPIDER BURROW.

NERD ALERT: COOL DIGS

LOTS OF ANIMALS BURROW. They may even try to conceal the entrances to their burrows. But building a door on hinges? That's something special. The underside of the trapdoor even has special holes that the spider can grab with its legs or fangs to throw the door open or hold it shut if an unwanted visitor comes by.

FUN FACT

A trapdoor spider lays silk "trip wires" near the entrance to its burrow. When unsuspecting prey touches the trip wire, the spider feels the vibration and jumps out of its burrow to grab its next meal.

FUN FACT

Trapdoor spiders are usually about the size of a U.S. quarter or larger. They're often dark brown or black and sport a glossy sheen.

CRITTER COSPLAY CLUB

WHAT IF ANIMALS GOT TOGETHER TO COSPLAY STAR WARS? CUE THE MUSIC AND IMAGINE A GALAXY FAR, FAR AWAY— RIGHT HERE ON EARTH.

FALSE MORAY EEL

NAME: Murray the False Moray Eel

SIGNATURE STYLE: Green glow

ROLE: Dreams of playing Princess Leia but always gets stuck being a light saber

MAY THE **FORCE** BE WITH YOU

AFFENPINSCHER

NAME: Fluffy the Affenpinscher

SIGNATURE STYLE: Luxuriously long locks

ROLE: Often plays an Ewok—but branching out as a Wookiee so she can go by "Chewie"

BATHYKORUS BOUILLONI

NAME: Dökk Bathykorus

SIGNATURE STYLE: Helmet-shaped bell

ROLE: Born to play Darth Vader—and nobody dare stand in his way

BINTURONG/BEARCAT

NAME: Tura the Binturong

SIGNATURE STYLE: Ear tufts, wise visage

ROLE: Yoda, the Jedi master—he even chuckles and grunts to get into the role

133

BASILISK LIZARD

YOU EXPECT TO SEE LIZARDS SCAMPERING AWAY FROM PREDATORS. BUT SCURRYING OVER WATER?
No way—unless you're talking about a basilisk lizard. Most of the time it hangs out in trees in Central American rainforests. At the first sign of trouble, it jumps down onto the water, stands up on its back legs, and takes off running where few predators can follow. The lizard's back feet have ridiculously long toes fringed with scale-like skin that spreads out in the water. It also pumps its legs superfast, creating tiny air pockets under its feet that help keep it from sinking. The lizard can sprint over water for a good 15 feet (4.5 m) before diving in and swimming—another of its athletic skills.

NERD ALERT: BEYOND BIZARRE

UNLIKE SOME TINY INSECTS, whose weight is supported by the surface tension of the water, basilisk lizards have to move crazy fast to keep from sinking. By pumping their powerful legs, they can cover five feet (1.5 m) a second.

DOLPHIN

A PLAYFUL, SMART, SMILEY FACE. There's a lot to love about a dolphin. But its best qualities come out in its pod, a group of five to 20 related females. Dolphins hunt together, form friendships that last decades, and teach each other new ways of doing things. One time, a female bottlenose dolphin off the coast of Australia grabbed a sponge from the ocean floor and stuck it on her snout. She used it to dig up prey from the seafloor without getting her snout scratched up. Seriously clever. It worked so well, she taught the skill to others. Now the sponge-users hang out with each other like they have their own sponge club!

NERD ALERT: BRAINY BEHAVIOR

JUST HOW SMART IS THE DOLPHIN? Its brain is big and complex—but very different from ours. That makes it hard for scientists to know for sure. What's clear is that these marine mammals have complex social networks, communication, and problem-solving skills, and can even understand symbolic language. All brainy stuff.

FUN FACT

Dolphins use echolocation, sending out clicking noises to locate things and to determine their shape and size.

FUN FACT

Each dolphin has its own signature whistle—like a name. Other dolphins learn it and use it to talk to—and about!—that individual.

PIGGYBACKERS

WHY WALK WHEN YOU CAN HITCH A RIDE ON YOUR PARENT'S BACK? THESE ADORABLE BABIES LIKE TO GET A LIFT.

HORNED MARSUPIAL FROG

THIS FROG MOM HAULS her eggs around in a pouch on her back, where her babies develop into little frogs—skipping the tadpole stage.

SWAN

WHAT'S BETTER THAN SNUGGLING UP in a down comforter? For baby swans, or cygnets, cozying up on a parent's back is a great way to warm up after a chilly swim.

CHIMPANZEE

A CHIMP MOM carries her newborn in her arms, but when the babe's grip gets strong enough, it hops onto her back and rides as long as it can get away with it—even for several years!

SCORPION

A MOTHER SCORPION carries her newborns on her back for 10 to 20 days. We're talking about a brood of as many as 100 scorplings!

CARRIER CRAB

AS CRABS GO, these guys are more on the spindly side, and their front claws aren't exactly impressive. So when it comes to protecting themselves, they may not have natural talent. No matter. They arm themselves with an urchin! Urchins are sea creatures with long, spiky, or venomous spines. And carrier crabs, as their name suggests, cart them around, using them as a protective shield against predators. The crabs have five pairs of legs (including their front claws), and the last pair in the back are adapted to lift and hold things on the crab's back. The crabs carry other things, such as coral or sponges, but urchins are their favorite load.

THIS CRAB SPORTS CORAL CAMOUFLAGE.

BRAINY OR BIZARRE? You decide. The crab needs some extra protection, so it snatches another sea creature and carries it around. But it's a win-win situation—a symbiotic relationship. What's in it for the urchin? A free ride to other feeding grounds.

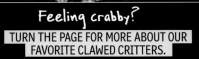

Feeling crabby?

TURN THE PAGE FOR MORE ABOUT OUR FAVORITE CLAWED CRITTERS.

"Crabby" means grouchy, ill-tempered, or spiteful—not something you want to be called. Even 500 years ago, people referred to grumpy acquaintances as "crabbed." Over the centuries, the word changed to "crabby," but it still was inspired by the way people viewed actual crabs: aggressive, snappish, combative. Why else would they painfully nip others with those big claws of theirs?

Another strike against crabs was the way many of them move: skittering sideways or backwards. People thought it looked like crabs were being evasive and unpredictable—another reason why "crabby" or "crabbed" was a useful way to describe difficult people.

These characterizations may seem terribly unfair to actual crabs, which are just doing their best to stay safe in this world. It turns out that figuring out a crab's true personality is rather difficult—not that researchers aren't trying. They've flipped crabs over, put them in new places, and showed them videos of predators—all to see how long it took the crabs to come back out of their shells. The findings have been mixed, but it seems that crabs are bolder in some situations than others and that some crabs are, indeed, bolder than others. No researchers have measured their level of grumpiness yet.

But that hasn't stopped people from referring to ill-tempered people as "crabby"—or depicting crabs as grouches.

FUN FACT

Male fiddler crabs have one large claw that they use for more than just fighting. They'll wave it around or drum it against something, in hopes of attracting a mate.

FUN FACT

Grumpy or not, crabs' claws are no joke. Coconut crabs are the strongest crabs, with a pinch nearly as powerful as a lion's bite.

TIGER SHARK

THE TIGER SHARK IS THE FOURTH LARGEST shark and the second most dangerous, after the great white. But when it comes to food, it's number one. This aggressive predator will eat anything that comes its way: lots of different fish and shellfish, seals, snakes, other sharks, or any dead animal floating around. You name it. With powerful jaws and serrated, or notched, teeth, it can saw through the toughest foods—even the shells of sea turtles. It prowls the ocean, moving systematically from the water's surface to the seafloor with one goal in mind: food. Sure, it might sound scary, but its ravenous appetite is a good thing. It helps keep the ocean's food chain in balance.

NERD ALERT: FAB FOODIE

TIGER SHARKS LIKE TO EAT, and they'll eat anything. Their reputation for being extremely unpicky has even earned them the nickname "garbage can of the sea." Unfortunately, in addition to actual food, they've consumed all sorts of trash that people have discarded, including license plates, shoes, and tires. One even ate a suit of armor.

FUN FACT

Female tiger sharks give birth to an average of 30 shark pups at a time—one even had 80! But the moms don't stay around to take care of their young.

FUN FACT

If a tiger shark doesn't look particularly stripy, it's probably an old shark. The stripes—which resemble the stripes of a tiger—fade as it gets older.

145

CROW

A CROW USES ITS TOOL TALENTS TO FIND FOOD.

THE CROW IS ONE OF THE SMARTEST BIRDS AROUND. It can solve problems, share safety tips with other crows, and remember where to go for a good meal. Researchers have discovered that in some ways, crows act as smart as human five-year-olds! Crows can shape things like sticks and twigs into tools to do certain jobs, such as digging food out of a hole. The birds also don't forget a face, and they even describe mean people to other crows so they'll be able to avoid them. So, the next time you hear *caw, caw,* just know: Crows may be talking about you!

NERD ALERT: BRAINY BEHAVIOR

A CROW'S BRAIN MAY ONLY BE AS BIG AS A HUMAN GROWN-UP'S THUMB, but that's huge in the bird world. Its smarts have allowed it to adapt to life in all kinds of places, even around us—as anyone who's seen crows raiding their trash cans can tell you.

FUN FACT

When one crow dies, others come to figure out what happened so they can avoid a similar fate.

FUN FACT

Hundreds of crows (and sometimes even up to a couple million) will gather together during the winter to sleep. In some places, they've roosted in the same area for more than a century.

DUNG BEETLE

ITS NAME MAY SEEM A LITTLE STINKY, but it's the perfect moniker for a bug that spends its life around poop—or dung, if you don't want to sound so gross. It rolls it up into a big ball, buries it, and lays its eggs in it. It even eats it. Most types of dung beetle live off the waste of plant-eaters, which don't digest their foods completely, leaving a nutritious, sloppy soup behind for the bugs. Many dung beetles are strong fliers and travel for miles in search of the perfect pile of poop.

FUN FACT

Ancient Egyptians, who viewed large dung beetles—or scarabs—as sacred, believed they kept Earth revolving, kind of like when they roll one of their big poo balls.

NERD ALERT: FAB FOODIE

DON'T DISS DUNG BEETLES. If they didn't do their jobs, we'd have a serious, smelly waste problem. Cows can drop up to a dozen piles of poop a day, and if the piles just sit there, they can kill plants and attract thousands of flies. Dung beetles take care of the poop before it's a problem. In parts of Texas, U.S.A., they bury as much as 80 percent of cattle dung!

FUN FACT

Besides the "rollers," some dung beetles tunnel below a pile of poop and arrange the dung in their tunnels. Others just climb onto a cow pile and lay their eggs inside it.

SHARK-CON

MOVE OVER, COMIC-CON. IMAGINE A LARGE CONVENTION THAT JUST CELEBRATES SHARK CULTURE. YOU MIGHT HEAR SOME INTERESTING TIDBITS FROM THE KEYNOTE SPEAKERS ON THE OPENING PANEL.

MEG A. DONETTE

TYPE: Great white shark

BIO: Star of Academy Award–winning movies and legends, Meg A. Donette is not simply the world's largest predatory fish. With a superior sense of smell and the ability to detect electromagnetic fields, she is taking on roles that showcase her complex nature.

OH, I'M SO HAPPY TO BE HERE WITH YOU, MY ADORING FANS!

AND **NOT** JUST BECAUSE YOU'RE TASTY.

HEY, HEY, WANT TO **SEE A TRICK?** LOOK AT ME! HEY, **LAST ONE** TO SWIM A FIGURE EIGHT IS A **ROTTEN EGG!**

I HOPE THEY DON'T HAVE JUST **TUNA AT THE BUFFET LUNCH** LIKE LAST YEAR.

SPOT

TYPE: Whale shark

BIO: Rivaling the size of a school bus, Spot is the largest fish in the world. She travels widely to teach others that, despite her five-foot (1.5 m)-wide mouth that could gobble up almost anything, she—like all whale sharks—only wants to eat tiny plankton.

GILL-BERT "SMOOTH MOVES" CARPENTER

TYPE: Scalloped hammerhead shark

BIO: Gill-Bert earned the nick-name "Smooth Moves" for his superior swimming agility, which he credits to his well-placed eyes and nostrils. He wishes to thank his schoolmates for jostling with him and sharing hunting tips.

BARTHOLOMEW SCUTE, JR.

TYPE: Wobbegong shark

BIO: Despite his superb skills as an ambush predator, Bartholomew Scute, Jr., has yet to gain the critical acclaim given to other sharks. The bottom-dweller's frilly beard and detailed camouflage make him disappear against the seafloor.

YOU KNOW, IT'S ACTUALLY **HARDER** TO CATCH FISH WHEN YOU'RE **HOLDING STILL.**

151

UP A TREE

SOME OF THE COOLEST ANIMALS IN FORESTS ARE HIGH UP IN THE TREE CANOPIES.

TREE KANGAROO

LIVING HIGH UP IN TREES, this cute kangaroo is so hard to find that locals sometimes call it the "ghost of the forests." The rare rainforest animal, native to New Guinea, sleeps about 60 percent of the time. A mom carries a joey in her pouch for eight to 10 months.

GREATER GLIDER

THIS FUZZY-EARED ANIMAL, which lives in eucalyptus forests in Australia, is a type of possum that glides using skin stretched from its knees to its elbows, giving it a triangular shape in flight. It uses its long, furry tail as a rudder to steer. Unlike other possums, its tail can't wrap around things to help it hold on.

TREE FROG

THIS RAINFOREST FROG hangs out in trees, thanks to super-grippy toes. Its toe pads have patterns that hold sticky mucus, and its last toe bones are shaped like a claw. With its fantastic feet, it can even hang on to wet or super-smooth surfaces with ease. Still not impressed? Some kinds of tree frogs can even change color, like a chameleon, to match their surroundings.

SPOTTED OWL

THIS GENTLE-LOOKING owl likes to nest in the hollow of an old tree. On a quiet night, its hoots can be heard a mile (1.6 km) away, but you won't hear it flapping about. It glides silently, swooping down to catch prey.

153

PYTHON

SOME PYTHONS—snakes native to Africa, Asia, and Australia—can grow to more than 30 feet (9 m) long. A python locates prey using its sight, smell, and special heat-sensing holes along its jaws. It waits until a small mammal, bird, or other critter is near and then grabs the prey with its teeth and quickly wraps its body around it. Then the python squeezes its prey—to death. If that doesn't send chills down your spine, get this: Joints in a snake's jaws are super flexible and its top and bottom jaws can move independently. That means it can open its mouths wide enough to swallow their prey whole—usually head first.

NERD ALERT: FAB FOODIE

PYTHONS DEFINITELY KNOW how to chow down. Depending on the size of the snake—there are around 40 python species of varying sizes—they eat anything from little rodents and birds to entire pigs and even antelopes. Once they eat, they can go for days, maybe even months, between meals.

155

HAIRY FROG

THIS IS ONE BIZARRE CREATURE. The African frog, which grows to about four inches (10 cm) long, stands out even among amphibians, a group of animals known for all sorts of unusual features. The male hairy frog grows long hairlike, fleshy strands along its flanks and thighs—probably to increase its surface area so its skin takes in more oxygen while it's underwater watching over eggs. But that's not the weirdest part. The frog can also pop claws out of its toes when it needs to defend itself. These aren't like kitty claws that naturally extend and retract. The frog's claws are actually bones that break through its skin. Ouch!

THESE FROGS HAVE CLAWS THAT WOULD MAKE PROFESSOR X PROUD.

NERD ALERT: BEYOND BIZARRE

MOST OF THE TIME A HAIRY FROG'S CLAWS AREN'T VISIBLE. They're tucked safely inside the frog's toes by a small bony bump. But when the frog needs to defend itself, it flexes a muscle that pulls each claw away from its anchor and lets it pop out. Bizarre.

FUN FACT

Hairy frogs are also called "horror frogs" and "Wolverine frogs"—the last nickname referring to the mutant X-Men hero.

FUN FACT

Scientists haven't figured out yet how the frogs retract their claws—if they can—or how their skin heals.

CRITTER HIGH
CLASS SUPERLATIVES

You're the life of the party.
Have an awesome summer!

 Glasswing B.

Most Talkative

THE AFRICAN GRAY PARROT has the gift of gab.
These supersocial birds live in huge flocks,
noisily roosting in rainforest treetops. They're
not only skilled at speaking their own language;
they're also top-notch impersonators. In fact,
African grays are often considered better at
mimicking human speech than any other kind
of parrot.

It was great hanging out with you this year!

—Sloth

NERDSVILLE CENTRAL: HOUTONG CAT VILLAGE

5 TIPS TO NERD OUT WITH THE CATS:

1 Houtong is an easy one-hour train ride from Taipei, the biggest city in Taiwan.

2 The village is split in two. A "cat bridge" leads from the train station to the kitties.

3 The cats are feral. Some don't mind playing and being pet, but others run away.

🚲 WHERE FELINES ROAM FREE

FOR CAT LOVERS, THIS IS *PURRADISE*. Houtong, on the island of Taiwan, is home to more than 200 freely roaming cats. They're everywhere. Cats of every color lounge under benches, on top of roofs, along hillside cottages, and even in flowerpots. The human residents couldn't be happier. A former coal-mining town, Houtong once had a population of 6,000 people. After the mines closed, its population dwindled to fewer than 100. By 2008, cats outnumbered people. Residents took care of the cats—even making sure they got their vaccinations and other health care—and let the world know that the village was a cat-friendly sanctuary. It didn't take long for cat-loving tourists to arrive. Signs with cartoon cats now adorn the village, and shops sell every type of cat-themed thing imaginable—and even play "songs" of cats meowing.

4 The cats are well fed, so it's best just to admire them.

5 The town also has a mining museum, a shrine, and hiking trails.

EDIBLE-NEST SWIFTLET

THIS LITTLE BIRD, a relative of the chimney swift, uses an unusual building material to make its nest: its own spit! Swiftlets, which live in countries along the Indian Ocean, produce long, sticky strands of saliva, which they layer onto the walls of caves or houses. The strands dry and harden, turning a whitish color. The edible-nest swiftlets keep adding layers of their spit until they weave a delicate-looking, but sturdy, cup-shaped nest that can hold a couple of their eggs. And yes, as their name suggests, the nests are eaten—by people!

NERD ALERT: COOL DIGS

MAYBE WE SHOULD say this bird has "tasty digs." In parts of Asia, swiftlet nests are used to make bird's nest soup—an expensive delicacy that can cost $100 a bowl—and other dishes. The nests are believed to provide nutrients and health benefits that help to improve concentration, slow aging, prevent cancer, and more. But they're not good for everyone; some people are severely allergic to them.

FUN FACT

In Asia, some farmers build empty houses and play recordings of swiftlet tweets to attract colonies of the birds to come and nest. The farmers "harvest" the nests after the swiftlet hatchlings leave.

FUN FACT

Edible-nest swiftlets use echolocation to catch insects— their favorite food— even in the dark of night.

163

GOING FORMAL

WITH THEIR FANCY DUDS, THESE ANIMALS LOOK SHARP ENOUGH TO TURN HEADS IN HOLLYWOOD. TAKE A LOOK AT THESE BLACK-AND-WHITE FASHIONISTAS!

SKUNK

IN CASE ANY animal needed reminding, the black and white stripes on this cat-size animal point to its sprayer, which can shoot out stinky spray up to 10 feet (3 m). Simply drawing attention to its smelly defense is sometimes enough to scare off predators.

BADGER

NAMED FOR THE WHITE MARK, or badge, on its head, this powerful critter has sharp claws to dig burrows and dig up food.

MALAYAN TAPIR

THIS DASHING ANIMAL can use its flexible snout as a snorkel when it swims. Despite its mini trunk and pig-shaped body, its odd number of toes indicates it's related to horses and rhinos.

GIANT LEOPARD MOTH

THIS EYE-CATCHING MOTH has a wingspan of about three inches (7.5 cm). The insect doesn't start its life with black spots. It transforms from a bristly black caterpillar with reddish stripes.

KOALA

A YOUNG KOALA—CALLED A JOEY—HANGS ONTO ITS MOM.

THE KOALA EATS NOTHING BUT EUCALYPTUS LEAVES, and it can put away about two pounds (1 kg) of them in a single day. Sound like a boring diet? Not to a koala! It's an expert judge on the quality and taste of leaves. There are more than 600 kinds of eucalyptus trees—all with a different taste—but koalas eat the leaves from fewer than 50 varieties. They also prefer the juiciest leaves from the tops of tall trees. Koalas live in the trees; they wrap their paws around the branches and sit wedged in forks in the branches. They need that comfy spot because eucalyptus leaves don't pack much energy. So, when koalas aren't munching leaves, they're sleeping—for up to 18 to 22 hours a day!

NERD ALERT: FAB FOODIE

KOALAS DON'T JUST LIKE EUCALYPTUS LEAVES; THEY'RE MADE TO EAT THEM. Eucalyptus is toxic to most animals. But koala moms feed their babies a special substance called pap. Pap gives the babies the bacteria they need in their digestive systems to handle eucalyptus, though sometimes they eat a little dirt to help their digestion.

FUN FACT

Koalas smell a little bit like menthol cough drops, thanks to strong-smelling oils in the eucalyptus leaves.

FUN FACT

You might hear them referred to as "koala bears," but koalas aren't bears. They're marsupials, pouched animals like kangaroos and opossums.

TRICK-OR-TREATERS

THESE SERIOUSLY SPOOKY SEA CREATURES ARE ALSO SERIOUSLY AWESOME. (BUT YOU PROBABLY DON'T WANT THEM RINGING YOUR DOORBELL NEXT HALLOWEEN.)

GOBLIN SHARK

WEARING A TOOTHY GRIMACE on its face, the goblin shark swims slowly through the deep, dark sea. When sensors on its long snout detect a nearby fish, squid, or crab, the shark's entire jaw shoots forward to spear its prey with its pointy teeth. Then it swallows its snack whole.

ZOMBIE WORM

THIS WORM, a member of the *Osedax* family, lives off the skeletons of whales and other dead sea creatures. It drills into bones with root-like structures and, since it doesn't have a mouth or a stomach, uses acid to dissolve the bones and get at their nutrients. It gets even weirder: The male zombie worms live inside the females. Yes, inside.

WITCH EEL

THIS EEL, ALSO KNOWN AS A DUCKBILL EEL, prowls the ocean floor looking for unsuspecting fish and shellfish to gobble up with its large mouth. Living in the tropical and warm temperate waters of the Atlantic, Pacific, and Indian Oceans, the grayish brown eel grows to four feet (1.2 m) long.

GHOST SHARK

THIS FREAKY FISH, also known as a chimaera, has creepy eyes—large, pale, and dead-looking—and a body that looks like it was stitched together by Dr. Frankenstein. While it's on the same family tree as other sharks and rays, the ghost shark branched off nearly 400 million years ago. This shark lives in the depths of the ocean, where there is no sunlight.

NO LANDLUBBER HALLOWEEN IS COMPLETE WITHOUT BLACK CATS. TURN THE PAGE TO FIND OUT WHAT'S UP WITH THAT.

WHAT'S UP WITH CATS AND WITCHES?

Any good witch worth her broomstick has a cat as a sidekick. Some of the best witches—hat tip to you, Professor McGonagall—can even transform into a cat at will. These cats aren't mere pets. In most stories, cats serve as witches' familiars—magical creatures with special bonds to the witches. At a minimum, they understand their witches and often assist them as lookouts or guides. Sometimes, the familiars even serve as the source of their witches' powers. Feline familiars have a long history. It was only during the Middle Ages in Europe—a time of unsettling changes—that the cats started getting a bad rap. Witches were blamed for all sorts of problems, including epidemics, natural disasters, and failed crops. During witch hunts, cats were seen as demon animals that helped witches cast evil spells and even feasted on the witches' blood. Before that time, familiars were viewed more positively, like guardian angels. Cats were linked to the divine and honored for protecting homes (from mice, if nothing else). The ancient Egyptians worshipped a cat goddess—Bastet—and from Japan to Russia to the Muslim world, they were viewed as bringing good fortune. Sure, there's nothing that says a witch can't have a parrot or even a pig for a familiar, and you even see the occasional witch's dog, owl, toad, or newt. But cats really make the purr-fect witch's companion.

FUN FACT

Cats were so important to ancient Egyptian homes that when they died, their owners would shave their eyebrows in mourning.

FUN FACT

In Japan, the *maneki-neko*—or beckoning cat—is a symbol of good fortune and prosperity.

GLASS FROG

FUN FACT

Glass frog tadpoles have bright red bellies.

THIS SPEC-TACULAR FROG HAS SEE-THROUGH SKIN ON ITS UNDERBELLY, giving you a good view of the organs tucked inside its body—even, in some species, its dark-red beating heart. Scientists aren't sure if the see-through skin helps the frog in any way, other than looking cool. The bumpy patterns on its back—large, round yellow spots on an apple green background—look like a bunch of glass frog eggs. So if a predator, like a wasp, comes near, male frogs can use their eggy camouflage to confuse it and lure it away from the real eggs.

FUN FACT

The glass frog grows about as long as the diameter of a U.S. quarter, with its head taking up more than a third of that length.

NERD ALERT: Smart Style

A LOT OF FROGS come in dazzling colors. But these little glass frogs—which live in the rainforests of Costa Rica, Panama, Colombia, and Ecuador—show off a side we don't usually see!

CUCKOO

A WARBLER FEEDS AN IMPOSTER CHICK—THE CUCKOO!

A CUCKOO DOESN'T RAISE ITS OWN BABIES. In fact, it forces other birds to do it. Note the word "force." The other birds aren't volunteering. Instead, a cuckoo either tricks or bullies them into raising young cuckoos. The cuckoo mother picks a nest with eggs that look kind of like her own. Sometimes the cuckoo eats one of the original eggs and replaces it with hers when the nesting birds are away, but sometimes she just plunks one in—even when the nest's original owners are trying to fight her off. Then, when the young cuckoo hatches, it either pushes the smaller birds out of the nest or hogs all the food.

NERD ALERT: BEYOND BIZARRE

EVER HEAR OF A PARASITE? It's an organism that lives off a host organism and gets its food at the host's expense. Generally, this is not a good thing for the host. Scientists call the cuckoo a "brood parasite." (A brood is a family of young animals.) From a cuckoo's perspective, it makes sense: It can put all its energy into making eggs, not raising them.

FUN FACT

There are more than 50 species of cuckoos, but it is only the common cuckoo that makes the famous *cuckoo-cuckoo-cuckoo* call that inspired the clocks.

FUN FACT

Cuckoo mothers often lay their eggs in the nests of the same kind of bird that raised them.

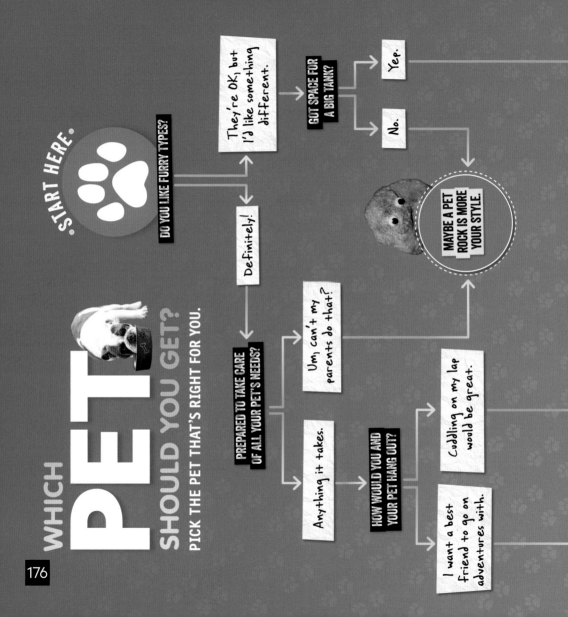

WHICH

PET

SHOULD YOU GET?

PICK THE PET THAT'S RIGHT FOR YOU.

START HERE.

DO YOU LIKE FURRY TYPES?

They're OK, but I'd like something different.

GOT SPACE FOR A BIG TANK?

Yep.

No.

Definitely!

MAYBE A PET ROCK IS MORE YOUR STYLE.

PREPARED TO TAKE CARE OF ALL YOUR PET'S NEEDS?

Um, can't my parents do that?

Anything it takes.

HOW WOULD YOU AND YOUR PET HANG OUT?

Cuddling on my lap would be great.

I want a best friend to go on adventures with.

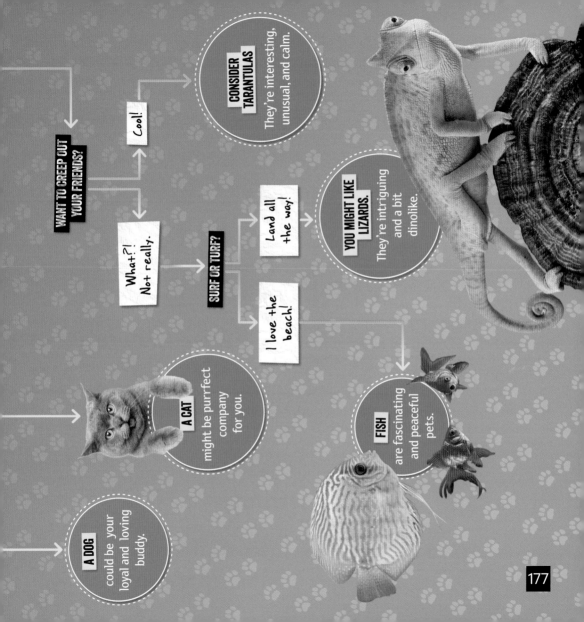

WANT TO CREEP OUT YOUR FRIENDS?

Cool!

CONSIDER TARANTULAS
They're interesting, unusual, and calm.

What?! Not really.

SURF OR TURF?

Land all the way!

YOU MIGHT LIKE LIZARDS.
They're intriguing and a bit dinolike.

I love the beach!

A CAT
might be purrfect company for you.

FISH
are fascinating and peaceful pets.

A DOG
could be your loyal and loving buddy.

LEAF ME ALONE

BLENDING IN WITH THE LOCAL FLORA IS A GREAT WAY FOR THESE ANIMALS TO ESCAPE NOTICE.

LEAF CHAMELEON

ONE OF THE WORLD'S SMALLEST reptiles, this little lizard from Madagascar virtually disappears in crunched-up leaves.

BRIMSTONE BUTTERFLY

THIS BUTTERFLY—found in the United Kingdom and Ireland—is all about camouflage. Its wings even have spots that look like tree fungus!

AMAZON HORNED FROG

THIS FROG'S MOUTH is wider than its body is long! Too bad for its prey, which it ambushes by jumping out of a pile of leaves.

GABOON VIPER

WITH A LEAF-SHAPED HEAD and coloring like the forest floor, this snake is hard to see—even though it can reach six feet (1.8 m) long.

OCTOPUS

TAKE ONE LOOK AT ITS BIG HEAD, and you might assume that the octopus is a brainy creature. You'd be right—but also kinda wrong. The octopus is, indeed, smart. It solves problems, uses tools, learns by watching others, and recognizes people. It has a big brain and a complex nervous system with almost as many brainy nerve cells, or neurons, as dogs have. But its nervous system is way different from ours (or a dog's). It's spread out, with 60 percent of the neurons in its arms, not its head! It's like its arms have minds of their own. One might be figuring out how to crack into a crab, while the rest of the animal goes about searching for its next snack.

OCTOPUSES SOMETIMES CARRY EMPTY SHELLS TO HIDE IN.

NERD ALERT: BRAINY BEHAVIOR

BECAUSE ITS BRAIN AND NERVOUS SYSTEM are so different from those of other animals, it's hard to figure out just how smart the octopus actually is. A sign of intelligence is coming up with new ways of doing things, and octopuses are masters at that. They solve puzzles and even figure out how to escape their tanks at aquariums.

FUN FACT

With few hard parts in its body, the octopus is a serious shape-shifter. It can squeeze through a hole not much larger than one of its eyes.

FUN FACT

Not only do octopuses have strange nervous systems, they also have three hearts and blue-green blood.

PINK LAND IGUANA

SEVERAL UNUSUAL TYPES OF IGUANAS live on the Galápagos Islands, but few rock the style of the pink land iguana. This iguana really does have a rosy pink head and a pink-and-black body, often with cool black stripes. First thinking the iguana was an oddity, scientists figured out that it's an entirely different species. These iguanas live in only one place: the northern flank of the Wolf Volcano on Isabela, the largest island in the Galápagos. During the rainy season, December through June, they live high up in shrublands near the volcano's crater. They come down to forested areas during the dry season. It's a risky existence because Wolf is an active volcano.

WOLF VOLCANO, AKA PINK LAND IGUANA PARADISE

NERD ALERT: COOL DIGS

THE GALÁPAGOS ISLANDS OFF THE COAST OF ECUADOR are home to all sorts of amazing plants and animals—it's a unique habitat created by the islands' isolation, their location near where three ocean currents come together, and volcanic activity. Every animal living in the Galápagos has cool digs. But living on a volcano? That's something really special.

FUN FACT

To attract mates, a male pink land iguana bobs his head up and down three times within four to five seconds. It's not unusual for male iguanas to bob their head, but these do it a lot faster than others.

FUN FACT

The iguana's pink coloring is actually because it has little skin pigment. The blood circulating under its skin provides the pinkish tint.

THINK YOU CAN DANCE

YOU MAY THINK YOU HAVE SOME SWEET MOVES, BUT SOME ANIMALS REALLY TEAR UP THE DANCE FLOOR.

PEACOCK SPIDER

THIS LITTLE SPIDER DANCES LIKE ITS LIFE DEPENDS ON IT— and it usually does. The male peacock spider has colorful tail flaps that he raises up behind it like a peacock tail. He swings them around, hops about, and waves his legs at the ladies. If a female doesn't like the dance, she kills the male. Even if she does like the dance, she may kill the male anyway.

HUMPBACK WHALE

WHAT ROMANTICS THESE WHALES ARE! To find his ladylove, a male will sing haunting songs. Once he attracts a female, they swim side by side in a graceful waltz—unless other males show up. Then the males engage in a showy battle that involves leaping out of the water and body-slamming each other until one is triumphant.

BIRD-OF-PARADISE

NO ANIMAL OUTDANCES a male bird-of-paradise. This bird—there are 39 species living in the rainforests of New Guinea—has all kinds of moves to impress potential mates. It spreads feathers into umbrella shapes, bobs its head, hops back and forth, flashes sparkling colors, and even flips its feathers into a smiley face.

MUDSKIPPER

THIS DIRTY BUT DAZZLING FISH can breathe air and spends most of its time on mudflats. It has leg-like fins, so it can walk out of the water. But its most impressive move—designed to attract mates—is leaping a foot and a half (0.5 m) into the air and then flopping down sideways onto the mud.

Don't stop the music!
FIND OUT HOW TO HARNESS NATURE'S DANCE MOVES FROM THE NERD OF NOTE ON THE NEXT PAGE.

185

If anyone knows how to bring out your inner feline, it's Clare Rickard. She not only starred as one of the cats in a London production of the musical *Cats*, but she was also dance captain, helping to teach cat moves to other actors.

Cats, based on poet T.S. Eliot's *Old Possum's Book of Practical Cats*, is one of the most popular musicals ever—but it demands a lot from actors. It's not just that it takes up to two hours of makeup and costuming to get the cat look. Actors also have to sing and dance in a cat-like way. "Cats express a lot of feelings through their bodies," Clare explains. They arch their backs and angle their heads and bodies to show a range of emotions, from joy to fear to anger.

It's not easy for a human to mimic a four-legged animal. But each actor makes it believable. They tuck their belly up, arch their back really high, and then lift their chest up. The actors rub heads against each other and twitch their noses. They work on every detail, all the way down to their paws. Instead of just lifting their hands, the actors first lift the whole arm, letting their hands curl into paws in a fluid motion. As dance captain, Clare learned every role in the musical and made sure everyone got their moves right, so they seemed cat-like, whether they were crawling on all fours or dancing on two legs.

"I grew up with cats. I'm much more of a cat person than a dog person. I love their nature and the way they can be aloof one minute and your best friend the next."

CLARE RICKARD, actor, dance captain

SHORT-HORNED LIZARD

EVERYTHING ABOUT THIS LIZARD SAYS, *DON'T MESS WITH ME!* If its camouflage doesn't disguise it, its looks are meant to stop a predator in its tracks. First, there's the crown of spikes around the back of its head. Then there are the spikes—actually short, pointy scales—that run along the edges of its body. If danger still threatens, the lizard can inflate itself to almost twice its normal size—which is really hard to fit into a mouth. If big cats or canids (dogs, wolves, coyotes) come after it, the lizard has an even more extreme defense: It squirts blood from its eyes! The blood can travel up to six feet (1.8 m), and canids find it especially disgusting.

NERD ALERT: BEYOND BIZARRE

THIS LIZARD, which lives throughout North and Central America, eat ants—a lot of ants. To get enough nutrition, it has to fill its big stomach. But it's tough to flee from predators with a big, full stomach, so ... blood squirting.

The horned lizard coats ants with a thick mucus from the back of its throat. It protects the lizard from ant stings as it swallows the insects.

NERDSVILLE CENTRAL:
THE KANGAROO SANCTUARY

1 The sanctuary is located outside the town of Alice Springs in central Australia; sanctuary staff pick you up in the town.

2 Sunset tours—the only way to see the kangaroos—sell out fast, so it's best to book in advance.

AN OUTBACK OASIS

NOTHING SAYS "AUSTRALIA" LIKE A KANGAROO. This powerful animal, which stands as tall as a human grown-up, is the only large mammal that gets around by hopping—and it is outstanding at it! A kangaroo can leap 30 feet (9 m) in a single bound. Sometimes kangaroos get hurt or are orphaned, and that's where the Kangaroo Sanctuary comes in. It rescues and cares for kangaroos—including babies, or joeys—and, whenever possible, releases them back into the wild. Any kangaroo that can't be returned to the wild continues to live in the sanctuary's 188-acre (76-ha) wildlife preserve in the Australian outback. The sanctuary started as a baby kangaroo rescue center but added the large preserve and a wildlife hospital. Kangaroo lovers can tour the sanctuary, see the kangaroos in their natural habitat—including some kangaroos that starred in the documentary *Kangaroo Dundee*—and get up close and personal with little joeys. That is an opportunity worth jumping at!

3 TIPS TO NERD OUT WITH THE KANGAROOS:

3 Be quiet and stay on the paths so you don't scare the kangaroos.

GIANT ANTEATER

THIS STREAMLINED ANIMAL with cool racing stripes is superfast—with its tongue, that is. It can flick it in and out of its mouth 150 times in a single minute. Why would it want to do that? To slurp up ants and termites. The giant anteater is fantastically suited for getting its favorite foods. It locates ants and termites—and can even tell what species they are—with its fantastic sense of smell. When it finds a nest, it tears into it with its sharp front claws. Then the anteater pokes its long, skinny head in and goes to work. Its tongue is two feet (60 cm) long and has teeny spines covered with sticky saliva—perfect for snaring insects.

NERD ALERT: FAB FOODIE

THESE GREYHOUND-SIZE ANIMALS—native to Central and South America—are great meal planners. They only slurp up insects at a single mound for about a minute before moving on. That way, the insect colony can recover—making sure there are plenty of ants and termites for future meals.

FUN FACT

The anteater is a strong swimmer and uses its long snout like a snorkel to breathe when it's in the water.

CONE SNAIL

KILLER SNAIL. It's not a term you hear every day, but it totally applies to this sea creature. There are more than 3,000 species of cone snails, and like all snails, they're not exactly speedy. But these marine snails are armed and dangerous. A cone snail often will hide under the sand, sniffing the water with a tube-shaped siphon that sticks out of its shell. When an unsuspecting fish happens by, it harpoons it with another tube-shaped body part loaded with toxins. The toxins paralyze the fish, allowing the snail to reel it in and swallow it whole.

CONE SNAIL SIPHON

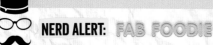

NERD ALERT: FAB FOODIE

THESE SLOWPOKES HAVE AMAZING ADAPTATIONS to ensure that they catch their next meal. The harpooning technique is pretty awesome on its own, but it's not enough. Thrashing fish might get away, so the toxins are needed to knock them out. The snails can also stretch their mouth really wide to fit around prey.

FUN FACT

Scientists are studying ways to use cone snail toxins to treat chronic pain and diseases, including cancer.

FUN FACT

The Hawaiian name for cone snails is "pūpū pōniuniu," which means "dizzy shell."

ANIMALIA ART SHOW

IMAGINE IF ANIMALS KNOWN FOR COLLECTING THINGS GOT TOGETHER TO SHOW OFF THEIR FINEST WORKS. TAKE A STEP INTO NATURE'S ART GALLERY—AND MEET THE GENIUS CREATORS.

IT'S NOT **MESSY.** IT'S **ECLECTIC.** GEEZ, I GET NO **RESPECT.**

PAT

SPECIES: Pack rat

FAVORITE MATERIALS: Mixed media—sticks, cacti, bones, human-made items

INSPIRATION: Creating a cozy home

ATOLLA JELLYFISH

THIS JELLYFISH, which lives deep in the ocean where sunlight doesn't reach, knows how to get attention. Normally a dark red, the Atolla jellyfish gets out of tough situations by summoning help. When a predator tries to eat it, the jellyfish produces a glaring alarm: glowing blue flashes of light that circle around like the lights on top of a police car. It's like the jellyfish is screaming, *Over here, over here. Come fast!* And who is the jellyfish summoning? A much larger predator—one that would love to feast on whatever is attacking the jellyfish. While the jellyfish's attacker freaks out about going from predator to potential prey, the jellyfish makes its escape.

NERD ALERT: Smart Style

A LOT OF DEEP-SEA MARINE CREATURES GLOW. They create their own light through a chemical process known as bioluminescence, but they don't all do it the same way or for the same purpose. The Atolla jellyfish's light display is especially clever—and has earned it the nickname "alarm jelly."

FUN FACT

The Atolla jellyfish has roughly 20 long tentacles along its body, plus an extra-long tentacle that may work like a fishing line, helping it trap food that floats by.

FUN FACT

A marine biologist created an electronic jellyfish—the E-jelly—that flashes an alarm like the Atolla jellyfish. Scientists use the E-jelly to attract deep-sea creatures so they can film and study them.

199

SPOT ON

"SPOT-ON" MEANS SOMETHING THAT'S EXACTLY RIGHT—AND IT'S A GREAT DESCRIPTION FOR THE COOL SPOTTED PATTERNS ON THESE WILD CATS. DO YOU KNOW THE "EXACTLY RIGHT" WAY TO TELL THEM APART?

CHEETAH

THE CHEETAH has plain, solid spots all over and black "tear marks" that run from the inside edge of its eyes down to the outside edges of its mouth.

LEOPARD

THE LEOPARD, THE SMALLEST of the big cats, has spots that are clustered together in flower-shaped groupings called rosettes. Some leopards are also black (and called black panthers): These cats are still spotted, but the spots blend in with the surrounding dark fur.

CLOUDED LEOPARD

THESE SECRETIVE CATS get their name from their irregular spots and blotches, which form in big cloudlike patterns.

JAGUAR

A JAGUAR'S SPOTS are clustered in rosettes, but there are spots in the center of the rosettes. Jaguars can also be black (and are also called black panthers) with hard-to-see spots.

Big into big cats?
SO IS THE NERD OF NOTE ON THE NEXT PAGE.

You might say that Thandiwe Mweetwa is lionhearted in more ways than one. Not only is she as brave as the big cats, but she loves them with all of her heart.

Thandiwe, a wildlife biologist and conservation educator, works to protect wild carnivores in the Luangwa Valley of Zambia, her home country. She and her partner track big cats and wild dogs throughout the African bush to make sure they're all right. She also teaches students about the animals and works with local farmers to decrease conflicts with wildlife.

It didn't take long to learn that tracking wild lions could be more exciting than she ever imagined. On her first day in the bush, her team wanted to put a tracking tag on a lion, but the tranquilizer dart didn't work completely. The lion woke up while they were tagging him. "I ended up having a staring contest with this young male for about two or three minutes before he could go back to sleep and we could continue working. It was an interesting first day of work!"

That experience might make some people rethink their careers—but not Thandiwe. It only made her more committed to protecting the magnificent animals.

"My job is one of the best on the planet. I get to see and touch animals that I'd only seen in books and magazines before—and it's an amazing experience."

THANDIWE MWEETWA, wildlife biologist

CRITTER HIGH
CLASS SUPERLATIVES

 Best Smile

WITH THEIR FRILLY GILLS AND PINK BODIES, axolotls are undeniably adorable. But what really seals the deal for these Mexican amphibians is their signature smile. And the cuteness doesn't stop there. While most amphibians go through metamorphosis, transitioning from their larval form to adulthood, axolotls retain juvenile features their whole lives. Talk about a baby face!

Your smile is infectious.
Thanks for a great year!!

—Sloth

Just keep swimming!!!

♥ Hippo

FRILLED LIZARD

WHEN THIS LITTLE LIZARD FEELS threatened, it unfurls large frills around its head. The frills, which are big flaps of skin, make it look a lot larger and a whole lot scarier. The frills pop open with the speed of an automatic umbrella, and the lizard completes the menacing look by opening its mouth wide and often by standing on its hind legs. The goal is to startle any creature hoping to snack on the lizard—giving the lizard time to sprint to safety, still on its back legs with its frills unfurled.

A FRILLED LIZARD SPRINTS ON ITS HIND LEGS.

NERD ALERT: Smart Style

THESE LIZARDS spend most of their lives up in trees in Australia and New Guinea. They flatten their frills and blend in with the branches. But when they come down to eat some bugs, they risk being eaten, too. That's when the frills come in handy. They even unfurl their frills when a rival lizard comes onto their turf.

207

BRILLIANT BUMS

WE HUMANS GENERALLY LIKE TO KEEP OUR BOTTOMS UNDER WRAPS. BUT SOME OTHER ANIMALS HAVE TUSHES SO TERRIFIC THAT THEY JUST HAVE TO SHOW THEM OFF!

WATERBUCK

IN CASE YOU MISSED IT, this big antelope's rump is ringed with a bright white circle. Some experts believe the white ring on a waterbuck's rear helps calves follow it when the herd is grazing or fleeing from danger. It's best to admire these animals from afar, though: Their sweat glands produce a stinky odor.

MANDRILL

THE MALE MANDRILL—INCLUDING ITS BIG PINK BOTTOM—IS BRIGHTEST when it ranks high in status in its monkey troop. Lower-ranking males' hormones change, which makes some of their colors fade.

WILSON'S BIRD-OF-PARADISE

HOW CAN YOU RESIST A TAIL that looks like one of those old-timey mustaches that curls up at the ends? For this rare bird, the male's twirly tail is just one piece of some serious swag. He also sports brilliant red feathers on his back, a turquoise cap, and a bright yellow patch on his neck.

DUCK

LUCKY DUCKS! Their derrières are darling— good thing, because many ducks are dabblers, nibbling on food in shallow water. To reach underwater treats, the ducks tip forward, thrusting their heads down and their tails straight up into the air. They even slowly wave their tails to help keep their balance as they dabble. Talk about a duck dance!

And that's the (REAR) end!

INDEX

Boldface indicates illustrations.

INDEX
CONTINUED

PHOTO CREDITS

214